Celestine Light
MAGICKAL SIGILS of
HEAVEN and EARTH

BY EMBROSEWYN TAZKUVEL

Celestine Light Magick Series

ANGELS OF MIRACLES AND MANIFESTATION
144 Names, Sigils and Stewardships to Call the Magickal Angels of Celestine Light

WORDS OF POWER AND TRANSFORMATION
101+ Magickal Words and Sigils of Celestine Light to Manifest Your Desires

CELESTINE LIGHT MAGICKAL SIGILS OF HEAVEN & EARTH

Secret Earth Series

INCEPTION *(BOOK 1)*
DESTINY *(BOOK 2)*

Psychic Awakening Series

CLAIRVOYANCE
TELEKINESIS
DREAMS

AURAS
How to See, Feel and Know

SOUL MATE AURAS
How Find Your Soul Mate & "Happily Ever After"

UNLEASH YOUR PSYCHIC POWERS

PSYCHIC SELF DEFENSE

LOVE YOURSELF
Secret Key To Transforming Your Life

22 STEPS TO THE LIGHT OF YOUR SOUL

ORACLES OF CELESTINE LIGHT
Complete Trilogy of Genesis, Nexus & Vivus

Celestine Light

MAGICKAL SIGILS of
HEAVEN and EARTH

Embrosewyn
Tazkuvel

Published by Kaleidoscope Productions
PO Box 3411; Ashland, OR 97520
www.kaleidoscope-publications.com
ISBN 978-0-938001-97-3

Cover design, illustrations & book layout by Sumara Elan Love

Disclaimer
Nothing in this book should be construed as medical advice.
If you have a health issue you should seek out a medical professional.

TABLE OF CONTENTS

INTRODUCTION

alling upon the higher realm power of angels, through intentional summoning using specific magickal sigils and incantations, is considered to be the most powerful magick of all. But there is a magickal method even greater. When you combine calling upon a mighty angel with adding synergistic sigils and words of power, the amplification of the magickal energy can be astounding and the results that are manifested truly miraculous. This higher technique of magick is the essence of *Celestine Light Magickal Sigils of Heaven and Earth.*

This is the third book of the Magickal Celestine Light series and is an intermediate level reference book for students and practitioners of Celestine Light Magick. It contains a melding of the sigils and names of 99 of the 144 Angels found in *Angels of Miracles and Manifestation*, coupled with synergistic sigils and magickal incantations found within *Words of Power and Transformation*. To fully be able to implement the potent combination of angel magick and words of power magick revealed in this book, the practitioner should have previously read and have available as references the earlier two books in the series.

When magickal incantations and their sigils are evoked in conjunction with the summoning of an angel for a focused purpose, the magickal results are often exceptional. The potent combination of calling upon angels and amplifying your intent with words of power and sigils of spiritual magick creates an awesome, higher magickal energy that can manifest everyday miracles. Employing this potent form of magick can convert challenges into opportunities, powerfully counter all forms of negative magick, entities, phobias, fears and people, greatly enhance good fortune, and help change ordinary lives into the extraordinary..

PART I

HOW TO USE THIS BOOK

1. Looking at the Table of Contents, choose the purpose or goal you wish to achieve and go to that link in the book.

2. In the center of the page is the sigil for the angel whose stewardship encompasses the purpose or goal that you seek. It will be the largest sigil on the page. Surrounding the angel sigil will be the sigils associate with words and incantations of power that are frequently useful to invoke in conjunction with summoning the angel, to increase the rapidity and amplification of the magick.

3. About 90% of the time you will find a synergistic harmony using all of the words of power and their sigils that are shown surrounding the angel sigil to most greatly amplify and achieve your purpose. However, sometimes you may decide that one or more of the words of power sigils are not synergistically appropriate for your specific purpose. If this is the case, and you have a printed copy of *Celestine Light Magickal Sigils of Heaven and Earth*, you should simply take a small piece of paper and cover up the inappropriate word of power sigil. You can do something similar on the screen of your eReader if you have a digital version.

4. There will also be occasions where you will find incantations and their sigils that are listed in *Words of Power and Manifestation* that you feel would be helpful in conjunction with summoning the angel for your particular purpose, but they are not shown on the angel page in *Celestine Light Magickal Sigils of Heaven and Earth*. In these cases, make a copy of the sigil you want to use, either with a scanner, a photocopier, or take a picture of it with your phone, and insert it in the circle of incantation sigils surrounding the angel sigil.

5. Once you have your sigil field set, either with the standard one shown in *Celestine Light Magickal Sigils of Heaven and Earth*, or in a custom field you have created by adding or deleting sigils from *Words of Power and Manifestation*, you are ready to begin coalescing and activating the magick.

6. Take some time to study each of the sigils carefully. Use your eyes to trace over the lines of the sigils. Every feature of the sigil summons some aspect of Celestine Light magick. The more you imprint the image of the various sigils in your mind, the easier it will be for you to coalesce the magick when you summon the angel or speak the incantations.

7. To successfully call an angel to your aid, you should review the detailed steps on pages 78-79 in *Angels of Miracles and Manifestation*. You should also reread Chapter 10 to fully understand how to interact with these powerful beings once you have summoned them. Some angels have specific incantations or actions that must be taken to successfully summon them. Whether they do or do not have specific incantation requirements, it is very helpful to look up the angel you are calling upon to be very familiar with them and the purpose of their stewardship before you call them. This will greatly aid your ability to establish a harmonic link with them through your heart, mind and psychic energy centers. The stronger your link is to the angel the quicker they will help you and the more amazing the results will be.

8. Assuming your purpose only requires a standard angel summoning, go ahead now and summon the angel. A rudimentary standard summons would be to say the name of the angel three times audibly, followed by this simple incantation:

Name, Name, Name,

Come to me.

As I need,

So let it be.

This should be repeated three times in entirety including repeating the angels name three times. Remember, the 'need' that you are summoning the angel for has to fall within their stewardship specialty. For instance, you wouldn't call upon Gwehwyfar, the Angel of Fertility, to help you develop your ability to astral project.

9. Once you have the angel in your presence and you are certain of that by your strong feeling of connectedness to the angel, either telepathically or by some other clear means of communication, succinctly explain the reason that you summoned them and specifically what you are asking them to do. As long as the purpose is good and beneficial, you can ask them to help someone else rather than yourself if you choose.

10. Next, begin invoking the words of power associated with the sigils surrounding the angel sigil. There is no correct order or sequence to which you invoke the first, last or in between. Whatever is your preference is the correct order for you at that time. Just like when summoning the angel, you should audibly say the words of power for each sigil three times. The power of your voice should increase each time you speak the incantation. For instance, if you were calling in the magick to *amplify your intuition* you would say:

Barkalon Dee! Barkalon Dee! **Barkalon Dee!**

Voice power is not simply saying the incantation louder, but saying it with greater passion, conviction and desire, which can also be accompanied by a louder voice if you choose.

11. That's it! You have successfully integrated the might of angels with the power of magickal Celestine Light sigils and incantations to coalesce far more powerful magick to aid you in your quest than either would have manifested alone.

FURTHER ELABORATION UPON POINTS 3 AND 4

s mentioned in points 3 and 4, there will occasionally be times when all of the Words of Power sigils that surround an angel sigil are not appropriate for a particular purpose. Covering them up so they are not viewed may seem simplistic and tedious but it is necessary. And there is no other way that adaptability could be built in to account for the many varied purposes someone may need. The same is true for occasions when a Word of Power incantation and sigil is not shown that in fact would be useful and need to be added to the conglomerate sigil illustration.

Here Are A Few Examples

1. If you were seeking a healing, you would summon the Angel Quanvera. On that page, surrounding Quanvera's sigil you will see the Words of Power sigils for: *#13 Turn Your Weakness Into Your Strength* and *#22 Attract People Into Your Life That Can Help You*, and *#44 Magnify Your Intuition*. These three sigil energies are beneficial in a wide variety of healing including physical, mental and emotional. If you feel one is not applicable in your situation you could cover up the sigil and not speak the incantation.

On the other hand, depending upon what type of healing you are trying to achieve, you may want to add one or more of the sigils and incantations found in sigil **#46 - #66** in the *Words of Power and Transformation book*. For instance, if a bad diet was causing you problems you would want to add *#46 to Increase Your Desire to Eat Healthier*. If you were suffering from Depression you would also add *#48 to Diminish Depression*. If you had the Flu you would want to add *#58 to Speed Healing from an Illness*. If you were more seriously afflicted with a disease of any kind, you would add #60 to *Accelerate Healing from a Disease*.

The Angel Lazon works specifically with energy healing and is the center of another sigil grouping that can often benefit from the addition of one or more sigils **#46-#66** in *Words of Power and Transformation*.

2. Magickal Defense is another purpose that is often enhanced by the addition of more sigils and incantations from *Words of Power and Transformation* as your specific need dictates. There are four sigils that highly enhance the purpose of Magickal Defense, regardless of what particular defense action is required. These four are shown with the angel sigil: *#2 Become More Passionate, #3 Become More Self Confident and Empowered, #11 Increase Your Ability to Focus on a Task*, and *#89 Coalesce, Concentrate and Amplify Your Auric Power*.

However, there are several others from *Words of Power and Transformation* that can also be very helpful depending upon your specific need. These include: *#80 Gain Whatever You Need to Overcome an Emergency, #81 Invoke a Circle of Protection from Psychic Attacks, #82 Invoke a Circle of Protection from Physical Violence, #83 Make an Antagonist or Adversary Lose Interest in You, #93 Discern an Energy Vampire, #94 Neutralize Negative Energy, #95 Reflect a Psychic Attack Back Upon the Attacker, #96 Create a Cloaking Bubble of Disinterest and Invisibility* and *#97 Make an Enemy or Attacker Afraid of You*.

UNUSUAL INCLUSIONS

here are some instances where you might wonder why a particular sigil and its incantation from *Words of Power and Transformation* is included in the array of sigils surrounding an angel sigil for a dedicated purpose. At first glance the connection to the purpose might seem tenuous or not even applicable. Remember, if you truly feel that is the case, you are welcome to cover up the sigil and not use it or its incantation as part of your activation of the magick for your purpose. Some of the more common instances that someone might wonder about are listed below with a short explanation of why they are included in the sigil array.

Nightmares

The sigil of the Angel Gualnthe is surrounded by sigils *#20 Become a Lucid Dreamer, #62 Sleep Peacefully* and *Get a Good Nights Rest,* and *#81 Invoke a Circle of Protection from Psychic Attacks.* Some people may wonder why #81 is included and how it relates to overcoming nightmares. Experience in the realms of magick for many decades has demonstrated that psychic attacks upon one individual by another are frequently the cause of nightmares. The attacks in most cases are not done with intentional magick, but are the unintentional consequence of one person's burning anger toward another. Though both people may be asleep at night, their psychic energy centers are often very active and involved in their night time dream experiences. A psychic energy cord connection is made between the two sleeping individuals that can definitely manifest as nightmares. Though this will not always be the cause of nightmares, it is the cause frequently enough to warrant including the sigil and incantation to ward off psychic attacks.

Optimism

Centered by the sigil of the Angel Vohumanah, the surrounding array of *Words of Power and Transformation* sigils includes *#9 Increase Your Luck, #47 Diminish Anxiety, Fear and Worry, #48 Diminish Depression, #51 Stop Thinking Negative Thoughts, #52 Improve Your Mood,* and *#53 Attract More Positive and Supportive Friends Into Your Life.* Some might question the inclusion of #48 to Diminish Depression. If you desire to utilize the magickal array for Optimism and are certain you are not suffering from even a mild depression, you are welcome to cover up sigil #48 and not say the incantation. But please consider that many people experience mild forms of depression without even realizing or perhaps be willing to admit that depression is afflicting them. However often times, if someone is to the point that they need to invoke the magick to boost their level of optimism, it is not unreasonable that in many cases they also have at least a mild case of depression at that moment in their life. Because of this, #48 is included in the standard magickal array for Optimism.

Passion

Centered around the sigil of the Angel of Passion, Carmetisia, are the *Words of Power and Transformation sigils, #1 Become More Loving and Loveable, #2 Become More Passionate, #8 Become More Spontaneous and Playful,* and *#52 Improve Your Mood.* In addition to these four sigils, which have wide application in conjunction with the energy of passion, there are three other sigils of which one or more may be appropriate. These include: *#5 Become Less Critical, #26 Attract a Romantic Relationship,* and *#55 Heal Your Heart from an Emotional Wound.*

Let's Look At Why You Would Or Would Not Want To Include These Three Sigils.

- Becoming less critical is sometimes a necessary step to instilling more passion in your heart and life. If you are continually seeing your cup of life as half empty rather than half full, or if you find yourself thinking and/or saying negative things about family, friends and even people that you do not know, you will find that critical nature is a powerful impediment to being able to feel and exhibit more passion. If this is applicable to you, please include the sigil #5 in your magickal passion array.

- If your desire to have more passion is to enhance your likelihood of attracting a romantic relationship, you would definitely want to include sigil #26 in your magickal passion array. However, if you are seeking a different type of passion that has nothing to do with a romantic relationship, such as having a greater passion for your work, you would not want to include sigil #26 in the array.

• If you have been hurt in a romantic relationship in the past you may have built energetic walls around your heart that simply make it impossible for you to experience sustained passion. In many cases people with walls around their heart cannot experience passion even a tiny bit. If this is your situation, or the situation of someone you are coalescing magick for, then you absolutely need to include sigil #55 to eliminate the wall so the rest of the magickal energies in the array can have their beneficial effect.

Past Lives

The magical array for Past Lives is anchored by the Angel Ukolesqua and surrounded by *Words of Power* sigils *#12 Increase Your Spirituality and Closeness to the Divine*, *#19 Remember and Interpret Your Dreams*, and *#42 Communicate With Your Higher Self Using Automatic Writing*. Some practitioners of magick may question the inclusion of #12, especially if they are an atheist or agnostic. In contemplating this inclusion it is important to remember that we are working with Celestine Light magick, which inherently has a strong connection to the spiritual and divine. If someone has an aversion to the spiritual or divine they would probably find greater compatibility with a different school of magick.

Celestine Light teaches two forms of past lives – pre-existent in a tangible spiritual form with relationships, education and personal growth, and traditional reincarnation of dying in a physical life and having your essence and soul reborn at a later date into another body.

Pre-existent life is something every person that has ever lived experiences before they are born into their current life. Reincarnation from one physical life into another on the other hand, is more selective and is only necessary for those who, for one reason or another, never had the chance to have a full life of experiences and choices.

Regardless of whether one or both are pertinent to you, the inclusion of sigil #12 is always beneficial if you are seeking a greater connection to the knowledge, experiences and relationships you had before the life you are currently living.

Survival

When someone is in a survival mode due to the circumstances of their life there are many supporting *Words of Power* sigils that are always helpful to include in the magickal summoning array. These include *#4 Become More Balanced, #6 Become More Discerning, #11 Increase Your Ability to focus on a Task, #13 Turn Your Weakness Into Your Strength, #47 Diminish Anxiety, Fear & Worry, #51 Stop Thinking Negative Thoughts,* and *#80 Gain Whatever You Need to Overcome an Emergency.* Additionally, there are four sigils that while not included in the standard array are often very useful.

Optional inclusions depending upon the circumstances include: *#18 Be Able to Accomplish More in Less Time, #37 Reveal a Person's Hidden Agenda, #50 Diminish Physical Pain* and *#88 Rapidly Change Your Life's Reality.*

If your emergency depends upon needing to take a decisive action or make a dramatic change in a very short period of time you should add #18 to the magickal array.

If you know or suspect that a particular person has it in for you and is the behind-the-scenes cause of your problems, you should invoke sigil #37 to make their hidden agenda obvious. This alone can sometimes overcome the problem as the last thing a secret adversary wants is to be revealed as an adversary, since they often times masquerade as a friend.

If you are physically suffering from pain of any source you should add sigil #50 to the mix.

Lastly, if your problem or challenge is bigger than just a particular emergency issue and involves the entire direction of your life, you should add #88 to the magickal array to help reorient your life to a more secure, rewarding and fulfilling path.

Wellness

The Angel Sálan has the stewardship of Wellness and she is a valuable angel to have as a friend and helper. If you maintain your body in a state of wellness, you will seldom, if ever, have need to call upon the Angel Quanvera for a healing. Creating and invoking a magickal array combining specific sigils from *Words of Power and Transformation* with Sálan's sigil creates a potent magickal force that can greatly contribute to your long-term state of wellness.

The recommended *Words of Power* sigils to add to the Angel Sálán's include: *#4 Become More Balanced, #13 Turn Your Weakness Into Your Strength, #14 Have the Willpower to Resist Temptation and Overcome Bad Habits*, and *#62 Sleep Peacefully and Get a Good Night's Rest*.

If the wellness challenge you are trying to conquer has anything to do with addiction, you should add sigil *#16 Overcome Addiction* to the magickal array.

THE MOST USEFUL MAGICKAL WORDS
OF POWER

There are 101 magickal incantations and power phrases in the book *Words of Power and Transformation* with accompanying sigils. Both the sigils and the magickal words are tailored to specific situations or goals such as *Becoming a Lucid Dreamer, Attracting a Romantic Relationship,* or *Increasing Your Luck*. But when used in conjunction with summoning an angel, certain words of power and phrases find application with far greater frequency than others.

Many of the sigils and words of power actually have little synergy with calling upon angels. Their purposes are simply too specific. For instance, *#28 Recovering a Lost Love*, or *#86 End a Dispute or Argument*, have very narrow parameters and are generally only useful for their specific purpose.

On the other hand, *#11 Increase Your Ability to Focus on a Task*, or *#89 Coalesce, Concentrate and Amplify Your Auric Power*, as examples, are useful in many different applications to achieve a wide variety of goals.

Following is a numerical list of the 101 incantations found in *Words of Power and Transformation* with the number of times that incantation and sigil are used in conjunction with an angel and their sigil in *Celestine Light Magickal Sigils of Heaven and Earth*. It would serve you well to become very familiar with the incantations and sigils that you see used a great number of times, even to the point of memorization. They have the adaptability to be very useful in many situations of life.

34 times ~ Turn Your Weakness Into Your Strength
33 times ~ Increase Your Ability to Focus on a Task
25 times ~ Become More Balanced
21 times ~ Become More Discerning

21 times ~ Become More Self Confident & Empowered
20 times ~ Coalesce, Concentrate & Amplify Your Auric Power
18 times ~ Become More Loving & Lovable
16 times ~ Easily Learn a New Skill or Talent
16 times ~ Stop Thinking Negative Thoughts
15 times ~ Communicate with Your Higher Self Using Automatic Writing
14 times ~ Improve Your Mood
14 times ~ Sleep Peacefully and Get a Good Night's Rest
13 times ~ Release Useless Guilt or Shame
12 times ~ Attract People Into Your Life That Can Help You
12 times ~ Become Less Critical
12 times ~ Diminish Anxiety, Fear & Worry
12 times ~ Magnify Your Intuition
11 times ~ Increase Your Spirituality & Closeness to the Divine
10 times ~ Be Able to Accomplish More in Less Time
9 times ~ Become More Passionate
9 times ~ Be Motivated to Stop Procrastinating
8 times ~ Attract More Positive & Supportive Friends Into Your Life
8 times ~ Be Better Organized
8 times ~ Become a Lucid Dreamer
8 times ~ Become More Intelligent & Retain Knowledge Easier
8 times ~ Become More Spontaneous & Playful
8 times ~ Have Willpower to Resist Temptation & Overcome Bad Habits
7 times ~ Discover Your Purpose in Life with a Vision of Your Best Path
7 times ~ Increase Your Luck
7 times ~ Remember & Interpret Your Dreams
6 times ~ Become More Aware and Comprehending of People's Auras
6 times ~ Rapidly Change Your Life's Reality
5 times ~ Make People Warmer to You
5 times ~ Propel Your Business or Project to Take Off
5 times ~ Unleash & Develop Your Creative & Artistic Abilities
4 times ~ Diminish Depression
4 times ~ Gain More Self Respect
4 times ~ Gain Whatever You Need to Overcome an Emergency
4 times ~ Heal Your Heart From an Emotional Wound

4 times ~ Know Other People's Thoughts
3 times ~ Become More Empathic
3 times ~ Encourage New Harmonious Friendships
3 times ~ Improve the Mood of the People Around You
3 times ~ Increase Your Physical Energy, Strength & Vitality
3 times ~ Calm Anger in Yourself or Others
3 times ~ Invoke a Circle of Protection from Psychic Attacks
3 times ~ Neutralize Negative Energy
3 times ~ Remember What You Study & Do Well On the Test
0 times ~ Increase Your Metabolism and Desire to Lose Weight
2 times ~ Activate & Enhance Your Ability to Astral Project
2 times ~ Activate Rejuvenation of Your Mind to the Quickness of Youth
2 times ~ Diminish Physical Pain
2 times ~ Discern an Energy Vampire
2 times ~ Have Your Talent Noticed By People That Can Help You
2 times ~ Invoke a Circle of Protection from Physical Violence
2 times ~ Motivate Someone to Become More Understanding
1 times ~ Activate Energy Inside of You to Heal Others
1 times ~ Attract a Romantic Relationship
1 times ~ Attract Your True Love / Soul Mate
1 times ~ Be Led to a Dimensional Doorway
1 times ~ Be Led to an Energy Vortex
1 times ~ Become More Clairvoyant
1 times ~ Erase a Memory You Do Not Wish to Remember
1 times ~ Have Money Come to You Unexpectedly
1 times ~ Increase Your Desire to Eat Healthier
1 times ~ Increase Your Income
1 times ~ Lessen Emotional Pain of Grief After a Loss
1 times ~ Motivate Someone to Become More Loving
1 times ~ Reconcile a Relationship Rift
1 times ~ Reflect a Psychic Attack Back Upon the Attacker
1 times ~ Reveal a Person's Hidden Agenda
1 times ~ Transfer Energy From an Enchantment Into an Object
1 times ~ Excel in a Competition
0 times ~ Accelerate Healing of a Disease
0 times ~ Activate Rejuvenation of Your Skin to a More Youthful State
0 times ~ Activate Rejuvenation of Your Body to a More Youthful

State

0 times ~ Attract Financial Support for a Project

0 times ~ Be a Better Public Speaker

0 times ~ Be Led to a Hidden or Lost Object

0 times ~ Initiate a Circle of Power

0 times ~ Create a Cloaking Bubble of Disinterest & Invisibility

0 times ~ Disinterest and Deflect Unwanted Attention

0 times ~ End a Dispute or Argument

0 times ~ End a Relationship Easily

0 times ~ Feel Motivated to Exercise

0 times ~ Levitate an Object

0 times ~ Make an Adversary or Attacker Afraid of You

0 times ~ Make Your Monthly Income Go Further

0 times ~ Motivate Someone to Become More Compassionate

0 times ~ Motivate Someone to Become Less Critical

0 times ~ Motivate Someone Stuck in a Rut to Change

0 times ~ Obtain Ideal Employment In Your Preferred Field

0 times ~ Overcome Addiction

0 times ~ Recover Lost Love

0 times ~ Turn Everyone's Focused Attention to You

0 times ~ Ensure Fair Legal Decisions

0 times ~ Speed Healing from a Physical Injury

0 times ~ Speed Healing from a Physical Illness

0 times ~ Start a Successful Business From Your Passion

0 times ~ Summon a Person to You or Lead You to Them

PART 2

PURPOSES TO MAGICKALLY ENHANCE

ABUNDANCE

ANGEL HUBERON (m)
hue-bur-ron
#17

Kazeez Vontour ~ #11
INCREASE YOUR ABILITY TO FOCUS ON A TASK
kah-zeez vohn-tour

Khronos Loquar Viviel ~ #18
BE ABLE TO ACCOMPLISH MORE IN LESS TIME
crow-nose loh-kwawr viv-ee-el

Jataash Wiseef ~ #22
ATTRACT PEOPLE INTO YOUR LIFE THAT CAN HELP YOU
jah-tahsh whis-eef

Vrans Xeka Korbose ~ #42
COMMUNICATE WITH YOUR HIGHER SELF USING AUTOMATIC WRITING
vrans zee-kah core-bohs

FEIZ NATHAAN ~ #69
HAVE MONEY COME TO YOU UNEXPECTEDLY
fee-eyz nahth-ahn

ORBANDA ALAMOZ ~ #70
INCREASE YOUR INCOME
ohr-bahwn-dah al-ah-mahz

VOLONDO PARTANA ~ #88
RAPIDLY CHANGE YOUR LIFE'S REALITY
voh-lohn-dah pahr-tahn-ah

ACHIEVEMENT

ANGEL SIJON (m)
see-jhahn
#18

KAZEEZ VONTOUR ~ #11
INCREASE YOUR ABILITY TO FOCUS ON A TASK
kah-zeez vohn-tour

KHRONOS LOQUAR VIVIEL ~ #18
BE ABLE TO ACCOMPLISH MORE IN LESS TIME
crow-nose loh-kwawr viv-ee-el

VRANS XEKA KORBOSE ~ #42
COMMUNICATE WITH YOUR HIGHER SELF USING
AUTOMATIC WRITING
vrans zee-kah core-bohs

BARKALON DEE ~ #44
MAGNIFY YOUR INTUITION
bark-ah-lon dee

FJAR SKOS ~ #67
PROPEL YOUR BUSINESS OR PROJECT TO TAKE OFF
fuhjahr skoss

QUIALANTRA KA ~ #72
BECOME MORE INTELLIGENT AND RETAIN
KNOWLEDGE EASIER
ki-ah-lahn-trah kah

ACTION

ANGEL VELITON (m)
vell-ee-tahn
#3

QOBAKON ~ #3
BECOME MORE SELF-CONFIDENT & EMPOWERED
qwhoh-bah-kon

KAZEEZ VONTOUR ~ #11
INCREASE YOUR ABILITY TO FOCUS ON A TASK
kah-zeez vohn-tour

ZOICE EXTOOZAR ~ #13
TURN YOUR WEAKNESS INTO YOUR STRENGTH
zoyce ex-too-zar

KHRONOS LOQUAR VIVIEL ~ #18
BE ABLE TO ACCOMPLISH MORE IN LESS TIME
crow-nose loh-kwawr viv-ee-el

ZONTA VARBON ~ #89
COALESCE, CONCENTRATE AND AMPLIFY YOUR AURIC POWER
zohn-tuh var-bohn

ASTRAL PROJECTION

ANGEL YAANIZANI (m)
yah-ah-nee-zah-nee
#92

Yisvas Xeoo Ekata ~ #45
ACTIVATE & ENHANCE YOUR ABILITY TO ASTRAL PROJECT

yhiz-vahss zee-oo eh-kah-tah

Qwasatar Ka ~ #74
EASILY LEARN A NEW SKILL OR TALENT

kwah-suh-tar kah

Zonta Varbon ~ #89
COALESCE, CONCENTRATE AND AMPLIFY YOUR AURIC POWER

zohn-tuh var-bohn

AURA

ANGEL AQUDIKAEL (m)
ah-coo-dee-kay-el
#93

ZDELANDA ~ #6
BECOME MORE DISCERNING
zee-deh-lahn-dah

KAZEEZ VONTOUR ~ #11
INCREASE YOUR ABILITY TO FOCUS ON A TASK
kah-zeez vohn-tour

YONTONA VAUSHAUN QZA ~ #41
BECOME MORE AWARE OF AND COMPREHENDING
OF A PERSON'S AURA
yohn-tah-nah vawsh-awn cue-zah

QWASATAR KA ~ #74
EASILY LEARN A NEW SKILL OR TALENT
kwah-suh-tar kah

ZONTA VARBON ~ #89
COALESCE, CONCENTRATE AND AMPLIFY YOUR
AURIC POWER
zohn-tuh var-bohn

BORMAI VORDAR ~ #93
DISCERN AN ENERGY VAMPIRE
boor-mey-voor-dar

BALANCE

ANGEL ZAESCHYLUS (m)
zays-chy-luhss
#56

QOBAKON ~ #3
BECOME MORE SELF-CONFIDENT & EMPOWERED
qwhoh-bah-kon

ZINGGNIZ ~ #4
BECOME MORE BALANCED
zing-guh-nihz

OPAROOM FANTESZAR ~ #17
DISCOVER YOUR PURPOSE IN LIFE WITH A CLEAR
VISION OF YOUR BEST PATH
oh-par-oom fahn-tess-zar

BLESSINGS

Angel Paschar (f)
paw-shar
#128

ZDELANDA ~ #6
BECOME MORE DISCERNING
zee-deh-lahn-dah

GAUSSA SABO ~ #10
RELEASE USELESS GUILT OR SHAME
gaws-sah sah-bow

ELOHIM JAKAXE ~ #12
INCREASE YOUR SPIRITUALITY & CLOSENESS TO THE
DIVINE
el-oh-heem jah-ka-zee

ZOICE EXTOOZAR ~ #13
TURN YOUR WEAKNESS INTO YOUR STRENGTH
zoyce ex-too-zar

Oparoom Fanteszar ~ #17
DISCOVER YOUR PURPOSE IN LIFE WITH A CLEAR
VISION OF YOUR BEST PATH
oh-par-oom fahn-tess-zar

Jataash Wiseef ~ #22
ATTRACT PEOPLE INTO YOUR LIFE THAT CAN HELP
YOU
jah-tahsh whis-eef

Jataash Mirakonda ~ #53
ATTRACT MORE POSITIVE AND SUPPORTIVE
FRIENDS INTO YOUR LIFE
jah-tahsh meer-ah-conda

Volondo Partana ~ #88
RAPIDLY CHANGE YOUR LIFE'S REALITY
voh-lohn-dah pahr-tahn-ah

CALM

Angel Leisyll (f)

lay-ee-see-el

#4

Jael Aladawon ~ #47
DIMINISH ANXIETY, FEAR AND WORRY
jah-el ah-lahd-ah-whon

Jael Markel ~ #48
DIMINISH DEPRESSION
jay-el mar-kell

Skoz Skalam ~ #51
STOP THINKING NEGATIVE THOUGHTS
skoz skah-lam

Lerylceon ~ #52
IMPROVE YOUR MOOD
lehryl-cee-on

Aashkadar Kuraz ~ #62
SLEEP PEACEFULLY AND GET A GOOD NIGHT'S REST
ahsh-kah-dar coo-rahz

Talialee ~ #84
CALM ANGER IN YOURSELF OR OTHERS
tah-lee-ah-lee

CAREER

ANGEL DALISCHER (f)
dahl-leesh-shair
#19

Qobakon ~ #3
BECOME MORE SELF-CONFIDENT & EMPOWERED
qwhoh-bah-kon

Zdelanda ~ #6
BECOME MORE DISCERNING
zee-deh-lahn-dah

Kazeez Vontour ~ #11
INCREASE YOUR ABILITY TO FOCUS ON A TASK
kah-zeez vohn-tour

Zoice Extoozar ~ #13
TURN YOUR WEAKNESS INTO YOUR STRENGTH
zoyce ex-too-zar

Khronos Loquar Viviel ~ #18
BE ABLE TO ACCOMPLISH MORE IN LESS TIME
crow-nose loh-kwawr viv-ee-el

Jataash Wiseef ~ #22
ATTRACT PEOPLE INTO YOUR LIFE THAT CAN HELP
YOU
jah-tahsh whis-eef

Barkalon Dee ~ #44
MAGNIFY YOUR INTUITION
bark-ah-lon dee

Fjar Skos ~ #67
PROPEL YOUR BUSINESS OR PROJECT TO TAKE OFF
fuhjahr skoss

STEEKA ~ #75
BE BETTER ORGANIZED
stee-kah

ZERAT TAKROK SIRACOSS ~ #77
HAVE YOUR TALENT NOTICED BY PEOPLE THAT CAN
HELP YOU
zehr-aht tahk-roc seer-ah-cahss

CHARACTER

ANGEL STRADANEL (m)
strah-duh-nel
#121

Qobakon ~ #3
BECOME MORE SELF-CONFIDENT & EMPOWERED
qwhoh-bah-kon

Zinggniz ~ #4
BECOME MORE BALANCED
zing-guh-nihz

Elohim Jakaxe ~ #12
INCREASE YOUR SPIRITUALITY & CLOSENESS TO THE DIVINE
el-oh-heem jah-ka-zee

Zoice Extoozar ~ #13
TURN YOUR WEAKNESS INTO YOUR STRENGTH
zoyce ex-too-zar

RA Q LON BARONDE ~ #14
HAVE THE WILLPOWER TO RESIST TEMPTATION AND
OVERCOME BAD HABITS
rah cue lohn bah-ron-day

JATAASH MIRAKONDA ~ #53
ATTRACT MORE POSITIVE AND SUPPORTIVE
FRIENDS INTO YOUR LIFE
jah-tahsh meer-ah-conda

CHOICES

ANGEL URARELIA (f)
yur-ah-rell-ee-ah
#58

ZDELANDA ~ #6
BECOME MORE DISCERNING
zee-deh-lahn-dah

RA Q LON BARONDE ~ #14
HAVE THE WILLPOWER TO RESIST TEMPTATION AND
OVERCOME BAD HABITS
rah cue lohn bah-ron-day

OPAROOM FANTESZAR ~ #17
DISCOVER YOUR PURPOSE IN LIFE WITH A CLEAR
VISION OF YOUR BEST PATH
oh-par-oom fahn-tess-zar

BARKALON DEE ~ #44
MAGNIFY YOUR INTUITION
bark-ah-lon dee

CLAIRCOGNIZANCE

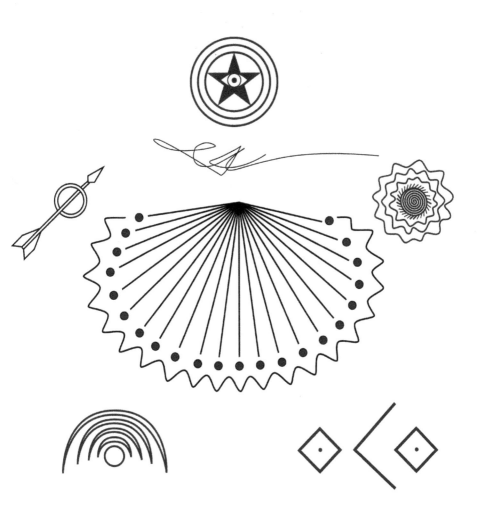

ANGEL ULALYANI (f)
uhl-ahl-ah-nee
#94

Zdelanda ~ #6
BECOME MORE DISCERNING
zee-deh-lahn-dah

Vava Kadong ~ #43
KNOW OTHER PEOPLE'S THOUGHTS
vah-vah kuh-dong

Barkalon Dee ~ #44
MAGNIFY YOUR INTUITION
bark-ah-lon dee

Qwasatar Ka ~ #74
EASILY LEARN A NEW SKILL OR TALENT
kwah-suh-tar kah

ZONTA VARBON ~ #89
COALESCE, CONCENTRATE AND AMPLIFY YOUR AURIC POWER
zohn-tuh var-bohn

CLAIREMPATHY

Angel Lavithal (f)
lahv-eh-thall
#95

ZDELANDA ~ #6
BECOME MORE DISCERNING
zee-deh-lahn-dah

WISPAUN HOOKAMBA SAI ~ #40
BECOME MORE EMPATHETIC
whis-pawn who-kahm-bah say

QWASATAR KA ~ #74
EASILY LEARN A NEW SKILL OR TALENT
kwah-suh-tar kah

ZONTA VARBON ~ #89
COALESCE, CONCENTRATE AND AMPLIFY YOUR
AURIC POWER
zohn-tuh var-bohn

CLAIRVOYANCE

ANGEL YATALIYAL (f)
yah-tah-lee-ahl
#96

Zdelanda ~ #6
BECOME MORE DISCERNING
zee-deh-lahn-dah

Wispaun Shalonz ~ #39
BECOME MORE CLAIRVOYANT
whis-pawn shah-lohnz

Qwasatar Ka ~ #74
EASILY LEARN A NEW SKILL OR TALENT
kwah-suh-tar kah

Zonta Varbon ~ #89
COALESCE, CONCENTRATE AND AMPLIFY YOUR
AURIC POWER
zohn-tuh var-bohn

COMPETITION

ANGEL ASKEGALL (m)
ahsk-ay-gahl
#5

QOBAKON ~ #3
BECOME MORE SELF-CONFIDENT & EMPOWERED
qwhoh-bah-kon

KAZEEZ VONTOUR ~ #11
INCREASE YOUR ABILITY TO FOCUS ON A TASK
kah-zeez vohn-tour

SHAMARIZ AKAWI ~ #85
EXCEL IN A COMPETITION
shah-mar-iz ah-kah-wee

CONTENTMENT

ANGEL ELLIQUEL (m)
el-lee-kwel
#70

JAMOVASAN ~ #1
BECOME MORE LOVING AND LOVABLE
jah-mo-vah-sahn

ZINGGNIZ ~ #4
BECOME MORE BALANCED
zing-guh-nihz

HOOVAUSH ~ #5
BECOME LESS CRITICAL
who-vawsh

JAEL ALADAWON ~ #47
DIMINISH ANXIETY, FEAR AND WORRY
jah-el ah-lahd-ah-whon

Skoz Skalam ~ #51
STOP THINKING NEGATIVE THOUGHTS
skoz skah-lam

Lerylceon ~ #52
IMPROVE YOUR MOOD
lehryl-cee-on

Aashkadar Kuraz ~ #62
SLEEP PEACEFULLY AND GET A GOOD NIGHT'S REST
ahsh-kah-dar coo-rahz

CREATIVE EXPANSION

ARCHANGEL SHIMWEMWE (m)

shim-whem-wee

#28

KAZEEZ VONTOUR ~ #11
INCREASE YOUR ABILITY TO FOCUS ON A TASK
kah-zeez vohn-tour

RABAA KALISH SUMAR ~ #21
UNLEASH AND DEVELOP YOUR CREATIVE &
ARTISTIC ABILITIES
rah-bah kah-leesh sue-mar

QWASATAR KA ~ #74
EASILY LEARN A NEW SKILL OR TALENT
kwah-suh-tar kah

DESIRE

ANGEL KALITHA (f)
kah-leeth-ah
#6

ZOICE EXTOOZAR ~ #13
TURN YOUR WEAKNESS INTO YOUR STRENGTH
zoyce ex-too-zar

ZEEATAR YAB ~ #15
BE MOTIVATED TO STOP PROCRASTINATING
zee-ahtar yahb

SKOZ SKALAM ~ #51
STOP THINKING NEGATIVE THOUGHTS
skoz skah-lam

LERYLCEON ~ #52
IMPROVE YOUR MOOD
lehryl-cee-on

LODOSH WIZTAR ~ #57
INCREASE YOUR PHYSICAL STRENGTH AND VITALITY
lohd-ahsh whiz-tahr

DISCERNMENT

Angel Jelehnessu (m)
jel-eh-nes-soo
#75

ZDELANDA ~ #6
BECOME MORE DISCERNING
zee-deh-lahn-dah

BARKALON DEE ~ #44
MAGNIFY YOUR INTUITION
bark-ah-lon dee

ZAKA WZRAMZEY ~ #82
INVOKE A CIRCLE OF PROTECTION FROM PHYSICAL
VIOLENCE
zahk-ah whiz-ram-zey

DREAM MEMORY

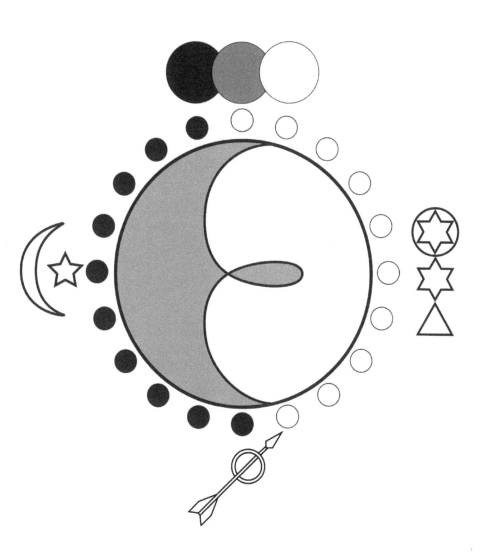

Angel Kaliisher (f)
kal-ee-ee-shur
#42

PEDLATZ ~ #19
REMEMBER AND INTERPRET YOUR DREAMS
ped-lahtz

HUMAR RABATZ Q ~ #20
BECOME A LUCID DREAMER
hoo-mar rah-bats cue

AASHKADAR KURAZ ~ #62
SLEEP PEACEFULLY AND GET A GOOD NIGHT'S REST
ahsh-kah-dar coo-rahz

QWASATAR KA ~ #74
EASILY LEARN A NEW SKILL OR TALENT
kwah-suh-tar kah

ELEMENTAL FORCE

Angel Yodacer (m)
yah-doh-uh-sair
#50

KAZEEZ VONTOUR ~ #11
INCREASE YOUR ABILITY TO FOCUS ON A TASK
kah-zeez vohn-tour

BARKALON DEE ~ #44
MAGNIFY YOUR INTUITION
bark-ah-lon dee

QWEX ZADATTA KABON ~ #64
ACTIVATE REJUVENATION OF YOUR MIND TO THE
QUICKNESS OF YOUTH
qwhex zah-daht-tuh-kah-bon

QUIALANTRA KA ~ #72
BECOME MORE INTELLIGENT AND RETAIN
KNOWLEDGE EASIER
ki-ah-lahn-trah kah

QWASATAR KA ~ #74
EASILY LEARN A NEW SKILL OR TALENT
kwah-suh-tar kah

ZONTA VARBON ~ #89
COALESCE, CONCENTRATE AND AMPLIFY YOUR
AURIC POWER
zohn-tuh var-bohn

ELEMENTAL POWER OF AIR

ANGEL LAHARIEL (m)
lah-har-ee-el
#48

ZOICE EXTOOZAR ~ #13
TURN YOUR WEAKNESS INTO YOUR STRENGTH
zoyce ex-too-zar

KHRONOS LOQUAR VIVIEL ~ #18
BE ABLE TO ACCOMPLISH MORE IN LESS TIME
crow-nose loh-kwawr viv-ee-el

BARKALON DEE ~ #44
MAGNIFY YOUR INTUITION
bark-ah-lon dee

LERYLCEON ~ #52
IMPROVE YOUR MOOD
lehryl-cee-on

Qwex Zadatta Kabon ~ #64
ACTIVATE REJUVENATION OF YOUR MIND TO THE
QUICKNESS OF YOUTH
qwhex zah-daht-tuh-kah-bon

Steeka ~ #75
BE BETTER ORGANIZED
stee-kah

Volondo Partana ~ #88
RAPIDLY CHANGE YOUR LIFE'S REALITY
voh-lohn-dah pahr-tahn-ah

ELEMENTAL POWER OF EARTH

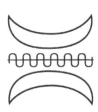

ANGEL BROMATI (m)
broh-mah-tee
#49

ZINGGNIZ ~ #4
BECOME MORE BALANCED
zing-guh-nihz

ZOICE EXTOOZAR ~ #13
TURN YOUR WEAKNESS INTO YOUR STRENGTH
zoyce ex-too-zar

JAEL ALADAWON ~ #47
DIMINISH ANXIETY, FEAR AND WORRY
jah-el ah-lahd-ah-whon

JAEL MARKEL ~ #48
DIMINISH DEPRESSION
jael-el mar-kell

JAEL OMERICSOL ~ #50
DIMINISH PHYSICAL PAIN
jah-el o-mehr-ick-sohl

LODOSH WIZTAR ~ #57
INCREASE YOUR PHYSICAL STRENGTH AND
VITALITY
lohd-ahsh whiz-tahr

ELOHIM OOTAME ~ #80
GAIN WHATEVER YOU NEED TO OVERCOME AN
EMERGENCY
el-oh-heem oo-tah-mee

ELEMENTAL POWER OF FIRE

ANGEL SHAZAR (m)
shuh-zhar
#51

JAAZ VAASHTATAN ~ #2
BECOME MORE PASSIONATE
jahz vaash-ta-tahn

QOBAKON ~ #3
BECOME MORE SELF-CONFIDENT & EMPOWERED
qwhoh-bah-kon

KAZEEZ VONTOUR ~ #11
INCREASE YOUR ABILITY TO FOCUS ON A TASK
kah-zeez vohn-tour

ZEEATAR YAB ~ #15
BE MOTIVATED TO STOP PROCRASTINATING
zee-ahtar yahb

Khronos Loquar Viviel ~ #18
BE ABLE TO ACCOMPLISH MORE IN LESS TIME
crow-nose loh-kwawr viv-ee-el

Aashkadar Kuraz ~ #62
SLEEP PEACEFULLY AND GET A GOOD NIGHT'S REST
ahsh-kah-dar coo-rahz

Fjar Skos ~ #67
PROPEL YOUR BUSINESS OR PROJECT TO TAKE OFF
fuhjahr skoss

Volondo Partana ~ #88
RAPIDLY CHANGE YOUR LIFE'S REALITY
voh-lohn-dah pahr-tahn-ah

ELEMENTAL POWER OF SPACE

ANGEL RAZANHAMISI (f)
rah-zahn-hah-mee-see
#52

Rabaa Kalish Sumar ~ #21
UNLEASH AND DEVELOP YOUR CREATIVE &
ARTISTIC ABILITIES
rah-bah kah-leesh sue-mar

Steeka ~ #75
BE BETTER ORGANIZED
stee-kah

Vavel Ondix ~ #98
BE LED TO A DIMENTIONAL DOORWAY
vah-vall ohn-dicks

Soolasee Graason ~ #99
BE LED TO AN ENERGY VORTEX
sool-lah-see grah-sun

ELEMENTAL POWER OF THE UNSEEN

ANGEL ISKKENEDER (m)
isk-kuh-en-uh-dehr
#53

Jataash Wiseef ~ #22
ATTRACT PEOPLE INTO YOUR LIFE THAT CAN HELP YOU

jah-tahsh whis-eef

Barkalon Dee ~ #44
MAGNIFY YOUR INTUITION

bark-ah-lon dee

Zaka Xeramzey ~ #81
INVOKE A CIRCLE OF PROTECTION FROM PSYCHIC ATTACKS

zahl-ah zee-ram-zey

Zonta Varbon ~ #89
COALESCE, CONCENTRATE AND AMPLIFY YOUR AURIC POWER

zohn-tuh var-bohn

BORMAI VORDAR ~ #93
DISCERN AN ENERGY VAMPIRE
boor-mey-voor-dar

TA RA ZERRAM ~ #94
NEUTRALIZE NEGATIVE ENERGY
tah rah zehr-ahm

TAKROTH XERRAMZA ~ #95
REFLECT A PSYCHIC ATTACK BACK UPON THE ATTACKER
tahk-rawth zehr-ram-zah

ELEMENTAL POWER OF WATER

ANGEL LACONDA (f)
lah-kahn-dah
#54

Zinggniz ~ #4
BECOME MORE BALANCED

zing-guh-nihz

Jeeteewee ~ #8
BECOME MORE SPONTANEOUS & PLAYFUL

gee-tee-wee

Zoice Extoozar ~ #13
TURN YOUR WEAKNESS INTO YOUR STRENGTH

zoyce ex-too-zar

Jataash Wiseef ~ #22
ATTRACT PEOPLE INTO YOUR LIFE THAT CAN HELP YOU

jah-tahsh whis-eef

Eizenhaar dlashmic ~ #25
ENCOURAGE NEW HARMONIOUS FRIEDSHIPS
eye-zen-haar dlash-mic

Jataash Mirakonda ~ #53
ATTRACT MORE POSITIVE AND SUPPORTIVE
FRIENDS INTO YOUR LIFE
jah-tahsh meer-ah-conda

Qwasatar Ka ~ #74
EASILY LEARN A NEW SKILL OR TALENT
kwah-suh-tar kah

ENCHANTMENTS

ANGEL WIZALARAY (m)
whiz-ahl-ah-ray
#98

KAZEEZ VONTOUR ~ #11
INCREASE YOUR ABILITY TO FOCUS ON A TASK
kah-zeez vohn-tour

ZONTA VARBON ~ #89
COALESCE, CONCENTRATE AND AMPLIFY YOUR
AURIC POWER
zohn-tuh var-bohn

RACSAA BINGALI TORMONDI ~ #100
TRANSFER ENERGY FROM AN ENCHANTMENT INTO
AN OBJECT
raac-saah bing-gah-lie tor-mahn-day

ENDURANCE

ANGEL TENAMIAH (m)
ten-uh-my-uh
#135

KAZEEZ VONTOUR ~ #11
INCREASE YOUR ABILITY TO FOCUS ON A TASK
kah-zeez vohn-tour

ZOICE EXTOOZAR ~ #13
TURN YOUR WEAKNESS INTO YOUR STRENGTH
zoyce ex-too-zar

SKOZ SKALAM ~ #51
STOP THINKING NEGATIVE THOUGHTS
skoz skah-lam

ELOHIM OOTAME ~ #80
GAIN WHATEVER YOU NEED TO OVERCOME AN
EMERGENCY
el-oh-heem oo-tah-mee

ZONTA VARBON ~ #89
COALESCE, CONCENTRATE AND AMPLIFY YOUR AURIC POWER
zohn-tuh var-bohn

ENERGY HEALING

ANGEL LAZON (f)
luh-zohn
#99

JAMOVASAN ~ #1
BECOME MORE LOVING AND LOVABLE
jah-mo-vah-sahn

ZINGGNIZ ~ #4
BECOME MORE BALANCED
zing-guh-nihz

JAAZ QBONDA ~ #61
ACTIVATE ENERGY INSIDE OF YOU TO HEAL OTHERS
jaaz cue-bohn-dah

ENTHUSIASM

ANGEL HAHATAH (m)
hah-hah-tah
#7

JAAZ VAASHTATAN ~ #2
BECOME MORE PASSIONATE
jahz vaash-ta-tahn

QOBAKON ~ #3
BECOME MORE SELF-CONFIDENT & EMPOWERED
qwhoh-bah-kon

LERYLCEON ~ #52
IMPROVE YOUR MOOD
lehryl-cee-on

LODOSH WIZTAR ~ #57
INCREASE YOUR PHYSICAL STRENGTH AND
VITALITY
lohd-ahsh whiz-tahr

Zonta Varbon ~ #89
COALESCE, CONCENTRATE AND AMPLIFY YOUR AURIC POWER
zohn-tuh var-bohn

EXCELLENCE

ANGEL QOLEGA (f)
kwoh-lay-gah
#76

Zinggniz ~ #4
BECOME MORE BALANCED

zing-guh-nihz

Kazeez Vontour ~ #11
INCREASE YOUR ABILITY TO FOCUS ON A TASK

kah-zeez vohn-tour

Ra Q Lon Baronde ~ #14
HAVE THE WILLPOWER TO RESIST TEMPTATION AND
OVERCOME BAD HABITS

rah cue lohn bah-ron-day

Zeeatar Yab ~ #15
BE MOTIVATED TO STOP PROCRASTINATING

zee-ahtar yahb

Khronos Loquar Viviel ~ #18
BE ABLE TO ACCOMPLISH MORE IN LESS TIME
crow-nose loh-kwawr viv-ee-el

Steeka ~ #75
BE BETTER ORGANIZED
stee-kah

FAITH

ANGEL ELCHIYUS (m)
el-chee-yus
#132

Zdelanda ~ #6
BECOME MORE DISCERNING

zee-deh-lahn-dah

Elohim Jakaxe ~ #12
INCREASE YOUR SPIRITUALITY & CLOSENESS TO THE DIVINE

el-oh-heem jah-ka-zee

Zoice Extoozar ~ #13
TURN YOUR WEAKNESS INTO YOUR STRENGTH

zoyce ex-too-zar

Oparoom Fanteszar ~ #17
DISCOVER YOUR PURPOSE IN LIFE WITH A CLEAR VISION OF YOUR BEST PATH

oh-par-oom fahn-tess-zar

FAMILY

ANGEL EPHILIAJEL (f)
ee-fee-lee-aj-el
#110

JAMOVASAN ~ #1
BECOME MORE LOVING AND LOVABLE
jah-mo-vah-sahn

JEETEEWEE ~ #8
BECOME MORE SPONTANEOUS & PLAYFUL
gee-tee-wee

TOLOI KLONDISH ~ #23
IMPROVE THE MOOD OF THE PEOPLE AROUND YOU
toh-loy klohn-dish

QSUN ~ #24
MAKE PEOPLE WARMER TO YOU
cue-sun

Wispaun Hookamba Sai ~ #40
BECOME MORE EMPATHETIC
whis-pawn who-kahm-bah say

Soolasee Ja Graason~ #55
HEAL YOUR HEART FROM AN EMOTIONAL WOUND
soo-lah-see jah grah-sohn

FERTILITY

ANGEL GWEHWYFAR (f)
gweh-wif-ahr
#59

JAAZ VAASHTATAN ~ #2
BECOME MORE PASSIONATE

jahz vaash-ta-tahn

ZOICE EXTOOZAR ~ #13
TURN YOUR WEAKNESS INTO YOUR STRENGTH

zoyce ex-too-zar

RA Q LON BARONDE ~ #14
HAVE THE WILLPOWER TO RESIST TEMPTATION AND
OVERCOME BAD HABITS

rah cue lohn bah-ron-day

COUPA ZING ~ #46
INCREASE YOUR DESIRE TO EAT HEALTHIER

coo-puh xing

LERYLCEON ~ #52
IMPROVE YOUR MOOD
lehryl-cee-on

FLEXIBILITY

ANGEL SRÉANAINN (f)
sray-ah-nay-in
#77

ZINGGNIZ ~ #4
BECOME MORE BALANCED

zing-guh-nihz

HOOVAUSH ~ #5
BECOME LESS CRITICAL

who-vawsh

JEETEEWEE ~ #8
BECOME MORE SPONTANEOUS & PLAYFUL

gee-tee-wee

FOCUS

ANGEL LARSARAI (m)
lahr-sah-rey
#20

QOBAKON ~ #3
BECOME MORE SELF-CONFIDENT & EMPOWERED
qwhoh-bah-kon

KAZEEZ VONTOUR ~ #11
INCREASE YOUR ABILITY TO FOCUS ON A TASK
kah-zeez vohn-tour

ZONTA VARBON ~ #89
COALESCE, CONCENTRATE AND AMPLIFY YOUR
AURIC POWER
zohn-tuh var-bohn

FORGIVENESS

ANGEL ALVATAR (f)
al-vuh-tar
#125

JAMOVASAN ~ #1
BECOME MORE LOVING AND LOVABLE
jah-mo-vah-sahn

HOOVAUSH ~ #5
BECOME LESS CRITICAL
who-vawsh

GAUSSA SABO ~ #10
RELEASE USELESS GUILT OR SHAME
gaws-sah sah-bow

ELOHIM JAKAXE ~ 12
INCREASE YOUR SPIRITUALITY & CLOSENESS TO THE
DIVINE
el-oh-heem jah-ka-zee

Toloi Klondish ~ #23
IMPROVE THE MOOD OF THE PEOPLE AROUND YOU
toh-loy klohn-dish

Valacot Kazrun ~ #33
MOTIVATE SOMEONE TO BECOME MORE
UNDERSTANDING
val-ah-kot kahz-ruhn

Dronda Jasalash ~ #36
RECONCILE A RELATIONSHIP RIFT
dron-dah jahsah-lash

Talialee ~ #84
CALM ANGER IN YOURSELF OR OTHERS
tah-lee-ah-lee

TA RA ZERRAM ~ #94
NEUTRALIZE NEGATIVE ENERGY
tah rah zehr-ahm

FRIENDSHIPS WITH ANIMALS

ANGEL DALAFARUS (m)
dah-luh-far-us
#111

JAMOVASAN ~ #1
BECOME MORE LOVING AND LOVABLE
jah-mo-vah-sahn

ZDELANDA ~ #6
BECOME MORE DISCERNING
zee-deh-lahn-dah

EIZENHAAR DLASHMIC ~ #25
ENCOURAGE NEW HARMONIOUS FRIEDSHIPS
eye-zen-haar dlash-mic

YONTONA VAUSHAUN QZA ~ #41
BECOME MORE AWARE OF AND COMPREHENDING
OF A PERSON'S AURA
yohn-tah-nah vawsh-awn cue-zah

Vava Kadong ~ #43
KNOW OTHER PEOPLE'S THOUGHTS
vah-vah kuh-dong

Barkalon Dee ~ #44
MAGNIFY YOUR INTUITION
bark-ah-lon dee

Zonta Varbon ~ #89
COALESCE, CONCENTRATE AND AMPLIFY YOUR
AURIC POWER
zohn-tuh var-bohn

GOOD DREAMS

ANGEL SAAJENDRALI (f)
sah-ahj-en-drah-lee
#43

Pedlatz ~ #19
REMEMBER AND INTERPRET YOUR DREAMS
ped-lahtz

Humar Rabatz Q ~ #20
BECOME A LUCID DREAMER
hoo-mar rah-bats cue

Yisvas Xeoo Ekata ~ #45
ACTIVATE & ENHANCE YOUR ABILITY TO ASTRAL
PROJECT
yhiz-vahss zee-oo eh-kah-tah

GOOD FORTUNE

ANGEL WIZMAR (m)
whiz-mar
#137

ISHSHATAR ~ #9
INCREASE YOUR LUCK

ish-shah-tar

JATAASH WISEEF ~ #22
ATTRACT PEOPLE INTO YOUR LIFE THAT CAN HELP YOU

jah-tahsh whis-eef

ZERAT TAKROK SIRACOSS ~ #77
HAVE YOUR TALENT NOTICED BY PEOPLE THAT CAN HELP YOU

zehr-aht tahk-roc seer-ah-cahss

ZONTA VARBON ~ #89
COALESCE, CONCENTRATE AND AMPLIFY YOUR AURIC POWER

zohn-tuh var-bohn

GOOD HABITS

ANGEL YENOVEFA (f)
yehn-oh-vay-fah
#78

ZINGGNIZ ~ #4
BECOME MORE BALANCED
zing-guh-nihz

KAZEEZ VONTOUR ~ #11
INCREASE YOUR ABILITY TO FOCUS ON A TASK
kah-zeez vohn-tour

ZOICE EXTOOZAR ~ #13
TURN YOUR WEAKNESS INTO YOUR STRENGTH
zoyce ex-too-zar

KHRONOS LOQUAR VIVIEL ~ #18
BE ABLE TO ACCOMPLISH MORE IN LESS TIME
crow-nose loh-kwawr viv-ee-el

STEEKA ~ #75
BE BETTER ORGANIZED
stee-kah

GRATITUDE

ANGEL SEVREEM (f)
sev-reem
#8

JAMOVASAN ~ #1
BECOME MORE LOVING AND LOVABLE
jah-mo-vah-sahn

ZINGGNIZ ~ #4
BECOME MORE BALANCED
zing-guh-nihz

HOOVAUSH ~ #5
BECOME LESS CRITICAL
who-vawsh

SKOZ SKALAM ~ #51
STOP THINKING NEGATIVE THOUGHTS
skoz skah-lam

GRIEF RELIEF

ANGEL ITAVIAH (f)
ee-tah-vee-ah
#138

GAUSSA SABO ~ #10
RELEASE USELESS GUILT OR SHAME
gaws-sah sah-bow

ZOICE EXTOOZAR ~ #13
TURN YOUR WEAKNESS INTO YOUR STRENGTH
zoyce ex-too-zar

JATAASH WISEEF ~ #22
ATTRACT PEOPLE INTO YOUR LIFE THAT CAN HELP
YOU
jah-tahsh whis-eef

JAEL ALADAWON ~ #47
DIMINISH ANXIETY, FEAR AND WORRY
jah-el ah-lahd-ah-whon

JAEL MARKEL ~ #48
DIMINISH DEPRESSION
jael-el mar-kell

JAEL JULANARI ~ #49
LESSEN EMOTIONAL PAIN OF GRIEF AFTER A LOSS
jah-el zhul-ahn-ahr-ee

SKOZ SKALAM ~ #51
STOP THINKING NEGATIVE THOUGHTS
skoz skah-lam

SOOLASEE JA GRAASON ~ #55
HEAL YOUR HEART FROM AN EMOTIONAL WOUND
soo-lah-see jah grah-sohn

AASHKADAR KURAZ ~ #62
SLEEP PEACEFULLY AND GET A GOOD NIGHT'S REST
ahsh-kah-dar coo-rahz

HAPPINESS

ANGEL SALLISELS (f)
sahl-lee-sells
#139

JAMOVASAN ~ #1
BECOME MORE LOVING AND LOVABLE
jah-mo-vah-sahn

QOBAKON ~ #3
BECOME MORE SELF-CONFIDENT & EMPOWERED
qwhoh-bah-kon

ZINGGNIZ ~ #4
BECOME MORE BALANCED
zing-guh-nihz

JEETEEWEE ~ #8
BECOME MORE SPONTANEOUS & PLAYFUL
gee-tee-wee

Jael Aladawon ~ #47
DIMINISH ANXIETY, FEAR AND WORRY

jah-el ah-lahd-ah-whon

Lerylceon ~ #52
IMPROVE YOUR MOOD

lehryl-cee-on

Jataash Mirakonda ~ #53
ATTRACT MORE POSITIVE AND SUPPORTIVE
FRIENDS INTO YOUR LIFE

jah-tahsh meer-ah-conda

HEALING

ANGEL QUAN VERA (f)
kwahn vair-uh
#73

ZOICE EXTOOZAR ~ #13
TURN YOUR WEAKNESS INTO YOUR STRENGTH
zoyce ex-too-zar

JATAASH WISEEF ~ #22
ATTRACT PEOPLE INTO YOUR LIFE THAT CAN HELP YOU
jah-tahsh whis-eef

BARKALON DEE ~ 44
MAGNIFY YOUR INTUITION
bark-ah-lon dee

HELPFULNESS

ANGEL SHALILTH (f)
shah-lill-th
#9

Jamovasan ~ #1
BECOME MORE LOVING AND LOVABLE
jah-mo-vah-sahn

Hoovaush ~ #5
BECOME LESS CRITICAL
who-vawsh

Zoice Extoozar ~ #13
TURN YOUR WEAKNESS INTO YOUR STRENGTH
zoyce ex-too-zar

Lerylceon ~ #52
IMPROVE YOUR MOOD
lehryl-cee-on

HIGHER SELF

ANGEL OARQUJAR (m)
oh-ar-que-har
#100

QOBAKON ~ #3
BECOME MORE SELF-CONFIDENT & EMPOWERED
qwhoh-bah-kon

ELOHIM JAKAXE ~ #12
INCREASE YOUR SPIRITUALITY & CLOSENESS TO THE
DIVINE
el-oh-heem jah-ka-zee

OPAROOM FANTESZAR ~ #17
DISCOVER YOUR PURPOSE IN LIFE WITH A CLEAR
VISION OF YOUR BEST PATH
oh-par-oom fahn-tess-zar

HUMAR RABATZ Q ~ #20
BECOME A LUCID DREAMER
hoo-mar rah-bats cue

HOPE

ANGEL IXCHEL (m)
eeks-chell
#140

Ishshatar ~ #9
INCREASE YOUR LUCK
ish-shah-tar

Elohim Jakaxe ~ #12
INCREASE YOUR SPIRITUALITY & CLOSENESS TO THE DIVINE
el-oh-heem jah-ka-zee

Jael Aladawon ~ #47
DIMINISH ANXIETY, FEAR AND WORRY
jah-el ah-lahd-ah-whon

Skoz Skalam ~ #51
STOP THINKING NEGATIVE THOUGHTS
skoz skah-lam

LERYLCEON ~ #52
IMPROVE YOUR MOOD

lehryl-cee-on

VOLONDO PARTANA ~ #88
RAPIDLY CHANGE YOUR LIFE'S REALITY

voh-lohn-dah pahr-tahn-ah

HUMOR

ANGEL KALPHRODILCIOS (m)
kal-fro-dill-cee-us
#10

Jamovasan ~ #1
BECOME MORE LOVING AND LOVABLE
jah-mo-vah-sahn

Jeeteewee ~ #8
BECOME MORE SPONTANEOUS & PLAYFUL
gee-tee-wee

Toloi Klondish ~ #23
IMPROVE THE MOOD OF THE PEOPLE AROUND YOU
toh-loy klohn-dish

Lerylceon ~ #52
IMPROVE YOUR MOOD
lehryl-cee-on

IDEAS

ANGEL JORENTIN (f)
jhoor-en-tin
#21

ZDELANDA ~ #6
BECOME MORE DISCERNING
zee-deh-lahn-dah

ISHSHATAR ~ #9
INCREASE YOUR LUCK
ish-shah-tar

KAZEEZ VONTOUR ~ #11
INCREASE YOUR ABILITY TO FOCUS ON A TASK
kah-zeez vohn-tour

HUMAR RABATZ Q ~ #20
BECOME A LUCID DREAMER
hoo-mar rah-bats cue

Rabaa Kalish Sumar ~ #21
UNLEASH AND DEVELOP YOUR CREATIVE &
ARTISTIC ABILITIES
rah-bah kah-leesh sue-mar

Vrans Xeka Korbose ~ #42
COMMUNICATE WITH YOUR HIGHER SELF USING
AUTOMATIC WRITING
vrans zee-kah core-bohs

IMAGINATION

ANGEL QALLIAS (m)
quall-lee-iss
#37

Kazeez Vontour ~ #11
INCREASE YOUR ABILITY TO FOCUS ON A TASK
kah-zeez vohn-tour

Rabaa Kalish Sumar ~ #21
UNLEASH AND DEVELOP YOUR CREATIVE &
ARTISTIC ABILITIES
rah-bah kah-leesh sue-mar

Vrans Xeka Korbose ~ #42
COMMUNICATE WITH YOUR HIGHER SELF USING
AUTOMATIC WRITING
vrans zee-kah core-bohs

Barkalon Dee ~ #44
MAGNIFY YOUR INTUITION
bark-ah-lon dee

QUIALANTRA KA ~ #72
BECOME MORE INTELLIGENT AND RETAIN
KNOWLEDGE EASIER
ki-ah-lahn-trah kah

INGENUITY

ANGEL YIZRÁDÁN (m)
yhiz-rah-dahn
#22

Zinggniz ~ #4
BECOME MORE BALANCED

zing-guh-nihz

Zdelanda ~ #6
BECOME MORE DISCERNING

zee-deh-lahn-dah

Kazeez Vontour ~ #11
INCREASE YOUR ABILITY TO FOCUS ON A TASK

kah-zeez vohn-tour

Fjar Skos ~ #67
PROPEL YOUR BUSINESS OR PROJECT TO TAKE OFF

fuhjahr skoss

QWASATAR KA ~ #74
EASILY LEARN A NEW SKILL OR TALENT
kwah-suh-tar kah

INTERLIFE CONNECTIONS

Angel Iustachys (m)
ee-oos-stahsh-ees
#123

KAZEEZ VONTOUR ~ #11
INCREASE YOUR ABILITY TO FOCUS ON A TASK
kah-zeez vohn-tour

PEDLATZ ~ #19
REMEMBER AND INTERPRET YOUR DREAMS
ped-lahtz

HUMAR RABATZ Q ~ #20
BECOME A LUCID DREAMER
hoo-mar rah-bats cue

VRANS XEKA KORBOSE ~ #42
COMMUNICATE WITH YOUR HIGHER SELF USING
AUTOMATIC WRITING
vrans zee-kah core-bohs

AASHKADAR KURAZ ~ #62
SLEEP PEACEFULLY AND GET A GOOD NIGHT'S REST
ahsh-kah-dar coo-rahz

KNOWLEDGE

ANGEL MOLCHÁN (m)
mohl-chahn
#23

KAZEEZ VONTOUR ~ #11
INCREASE YOUR ABILITY TO FOCUS ON A TASK
kah-zeez vohn-tour

QUIALANTRA KA ~ #72
BECOME MORE INTELLIGENT AND RETAIN
KNOWLEDGE EASIER
ki-ah-lahn-trah kah

VALAZIX KA ~ #73
REMEMBER WHAT YOU STUDY AND DO WELL ON
THE TEST
vah-lah-zix kah

QWASATAR KA ~ #74
EASILY LEARN A NEW SKILL OR TALENT
kwah-suh-tar kah

LEARNING

ANGEL EPHELIAOS (m)
eef-uh-lee-ah-ohs
#80

Kazeez Vontour ~ #11
INCREASE YOUR ABILITY TO FOCUS ON A TASK

kah-zeez vohn-tour

Zoice Extoozar ~ #13
TURN YOUR WEAKNESS INTO YOUR STRENGTH

zoyce ex-too-zar

Quialantra Ka ~ #72
BECOME MORE INTELLIGENT AND RETAIN
KNOWLEDGE EASIER

ki-ah-lahn-trah kah

Valazix Ka ~ #73
REMEMBER WHAT YOU STUDY AND DO WELL ON
THE TEST

vah-lah-zix kah

QWASATAR KA ~ #74
EASILY LEARN A NEW SKILL OR TALENT
kwah-suh-tar kah

STEEKA ~ #75
BE BETTER ORGANIZED
stee-kah

LEGACY

ANGEL JAELKAVEL (m)
jah-el-kah-vel
#60

JAMOVASAN ~ #1
BECOME MORE LOVING AND LOVABLE
jah-mo-vah-sahn

ELOHIM JAKAXE ~ #12
INCREASE YOUR SPIRITUALITY & CLOSENESS TO THE
DIVINE
el-oh-heem jah-ka-zee

OPAROOM FANTESZAR ~ #17
DISCOVER YOUR PURPOSE IN LIFE WITH A CLEAR
VISION OF YOUR BEST PATH
oh-par-oom fahn-tess-zar

QSUN ~ #24
MAKE PEOPLE WARMER TO YOU
cue-sun

LIFE PURPOSE

ANGEL LAKAJINAL (m)
lah-kah-gee-nahl
#61

ZDELANDA ~ #6
BECOME MORE DISCERNING
zee-deh-lahn-dah

OPAROOM FANTESZAR ~ #17
DISCOVER YOUR PURPOSE IN LIFE WITH A CLEAR
VISION OF YOUR BEST PATH
oh-par-oom fahn-tess-zar

PEDLATZ ~ #19
REMEMBER AND INTERPRET YOUR DREAMS
ped-lahtz

VRANS XEKA KORBOSE ~ #42
COMMUNICATE WITH YOUR HIGHER SELF USING
AUTOMATIC WRITING
vrans zee-kah core-bohs

LUCID DREAMING

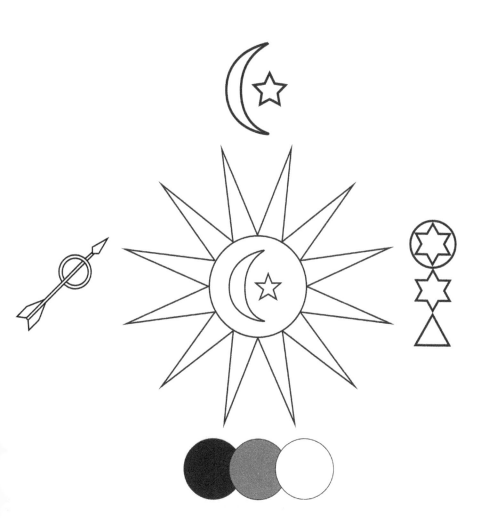

ANGEL OUDICAEL (m)
oo-dee-kah-el
#44

PEDLATZ ~ #19
REMEMBER AND INTERPRET YOUR DREAMS
ped-lahtz

HUMAR RABATZ Q ~ #20
BECOME A LUCID DREAMER
hoo-mar rah-bats cue

AASHKADAR KURAZ ~ #62
SLEEP PEACEFULLY AND GET A GOOD NIGHT'S REST
ahsh-kah-dar coo-rahz

QWASATAR KA ~ #74
EASILY LEARN A NEW SKILL OR TALENT
kwah-suh-tar kah

MAGICKAL DEFENSE

ANGEL AZKAEL (m)
az-kay-el
#101

JAAZ VAASHTATAN ~ #2
BECOME MORE PASSIONATE

jahz vaash-ta-tahn

QOBAKON ~ #3
BECOME MORE SELF-CONFIDENT & EMPOWERED

qwhoh-bah-kon

KAZEEZ VONTOUR ~ #11
INCREASE YOUR ABILITY TO FOCUS ON A TASK

kah-zeez vohn-tour

ZONTA VARBON ~ #89
COALESCE, CONCENTRATE AND AMPLIFY YOUR AURIC POWER

zohn-tuh var-bohn

MEDITATION

ANGEL DALEEN (f)
dah-leen
#126

ZINGGNIZ ~ #4
BECOME MORE BALANCED

zing-guh-nihz

ELOHIM JAKAXE ~ #12
INCREASE YOUR SPIRITUALITY & CLOSENESS TO THE DIVINE

el-oh-heem jah-ka-zee

AASHKADAR KURAZ ~ #62
SLEEP PEACEFULLY AND GET A GOOD NIGHT'S REST

ahsh-kah-dar coo-rahz

TALIALEE ~ #84
CALM ANGER IN YOURSELF OR OTHERS

tah-lee-ah-lee

MEMORY

ANGEL ULYVINDR (m)
yool-ee-vin-der
#82

KAZEEZ VONTOUR ~ #11
INCREASE YOUR ABILITY TO FOCUS ON A TASK
kah-zeez vohn-tour

ZOICE EXTOOZAR ~ #13
TURN YOUR WEAKNESS INTO YOUR STRENGTH
zoyce ex-too-zar

VALAZIX KA ~ #73
REMEMBER WHAT YOU STUDY AND DO WELL ON THE TEST
vah-lah-zix kah

NIGHTMARES

ANGEL GUALNTHE (f)
goo-all-inth-ay
#45

HUMAR RABATZ Q ~ #20
BECOME A LUCID DREAMER

hoo-mar rah-bats cue

AASHKADAR KURAZ ~ #62
SLEEP PEACEFULLY AND GET A GOOD NIGHT'S REST

ahsh-kah-dar coo-rahz

ZAKA XERAMZEY ~ #81
INVOKE A CIRCLE OF PROTECTION FROM PSYCHIC ATTACKS

zahl-ah zee-ram-zey

OPTIMISM

ANGEL VOHUMANAH (f)
voh-hue-mah-nah
#11

ISHSHATAR ~ #9
INCREASE YOUR LUCK
ish-shah-tar

JAEL ALADAWON ~ #47
DIMINISH ANXIETY, FEAR AND WORRY
jah-el ah-lahd-ah-whon

JAEL MARKEL ~ #48
DIMINISH DEPRESSION
jael-el mar-kell

SKOZ SKALAM ~ #51
STOP THINKING NEGATIVE THOUGHTS
skoz skah-lam

LERYLCEON ~ #52
IMPROVE YOUR MOOD

lehryl-cee-on

JATAASH MIRAKONDA ~ #53
ATTRACT MORE POSITIVE AND SUPPORTIVE
FRIENDS INTO YOUR LIFE

jah-tahsh meer-ah-conda

ORGANIZATION

ANGEL ALANTARIYA (f)
ah-lahn-tah-ree-yah
#84

Kazeez Vontour ~ #11
INCREASE YOUR ABILITY TO FOCUS ON A TASK
kah-zeez vohn-tour

Zoice Extoozar ~ #13
TURN YOUR WEAKNESS INTO YOUR STRENGTH
zoyce ex-too-zar

Zeeatar Yab ~ #15
BE MOTIVATED TO STOP PROCRASTINATING
zee-ahtar yahb

Steeka ~ 75
BE BETTER ORGANIZED
stee-kah

PASSION

ANGEL CARMETISIA (f)
kahr-meh-tee-zee-ah
#85

JAMOVASAN ~ #1
BECOME MORE LOVING AND LOVABLE
jah-mo-vah-sahn

JAAZ VAASHTATAN ~ #2
BECOME MORE PASSIONATE
jahz vaash-ta-tahn

JEETEEWEE ~ #8
BECOME MORE SPONTANEOUS & PLAYFUL
gee-tee-wee

LERYLCEON ~ #52
IMPROVE YOUR MOOD
lehryl-cee-on

PAST LIVES

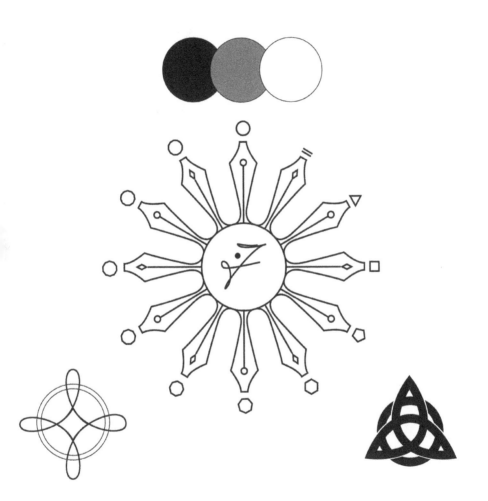

UKOLESQUA (f)
yoo-kohl-ays-kwah
#124

ELOHIM JAKAXE ~ #12
INCREASE YOUR SPIRITUALITY & CLOSENESS TO THE DIVINE
el-oh-heem jah-ka-zee

PEDLATZ ~ #19
REMEMBER AND INTERPRET YOUR DREAMS
ped-lahtz

VRANS XEKA KORBOSE ~ #42
COMMUNICATE WITH YOUR HIGHER SELF USING AUTOMATIC WRITING
vrans zee-kah core-bohs

PATIENCE

SARAYAVANUSH (m)
sahr-ah-yah-vahn-ush
#86

ZINGGNIZ ~ #4
BECOME MORE BALANCED

zing-guh-nihz

HOOVAUSH ~ #5
BECOME LESS CRITICAL

who-vawsh

QSUN ~ #24
MAKE PEOPLE WARMER TO YOU

cue-sun

YONTONA VAUSHAUN QZA ~ #41
BECOME MORE AWARE OF AND COMPREHENDING
OF A PERSON'S AURA

yohn-tah-nah vawsh-awn cue-zah

PEACE OF HEART & MIND

ANGELS COLOPATIRON (f) & NISROC (m)
koh-loh-pah-tee-ron & niss-roc
#136

JAMOVASAN ~ #1
BECOME MORE LOVING AND LOVABLE
jah-mo-vah-sahn

ZINGGNIZ ~ #4
BECOME MORE BALANCED
zing-guh-nihz

HOOVAUSH ~ #5
BECOME LESS CRITICAL
who-vawsh

GAUSSA SABO ~ #10
RELEASE USELESS GUILT OR SHAME
gaws-sah sah-bow

ELOHIM JAKAXE ~ #12
INCREASE YOUR SPIRITUALITY & CLOSENESS TO THE DIVINE
el-oh-heem jah-ka-zee

PERSISTENCE

ANGEL AUXALLIAS (m)
ox-zah-yill-ee-ahs
#87

QOBAKON ~ #3
BECOME MORE SELF-CONFIDENT & EMPOWERED
qwhoh-bah-kon

KAZEEZ VONTOUR ~ #11
INCREASE YOUR ABILITY TO FOCUS ON A TASK
kah-zeez vohn-tour

RA Q LON BARONDE ~ #14
HAVE THE WILLPOWER TO RESIST TEMPTATION AND
OVERCOME BAD HABITS
rah cue lohn bah-ron-day

ZEEATAR YAB ~ #15
BE MOTIVATED TO STOP PROCRASTINATING
zee-ahtar yahb

Skoz Skalam ~ #51
STOP THINKING NEGATIVE THOUGHTS
skoz skah-lam

PERSONALITY

Angel Praxistelos (m)
prahx-ee-stay-lohs
#88

JAMOVASAN ~ #1
BECOME MORE LOVING AND LOVABLE
jah-mo-vah-sahn

JAAZ VAASHTATAN ~ #2
BECOME MORE PASSIONATE
jahz vaash-ta-tahn

QOBAKON ~ #3
BECOME MORE SELF-CONFIDENT & EMPOWERED
qwhoh-bah-kon

ZINGGNIZ ~ #4
BECOME MORE BALANCED
zing-guh-nihz

Hoovaush ~ #5
BECOME LESS CRITICAL
who-vawsh

Jeeteewee ~ #8
BECOME MORE SPONTANEOUS & PLAYFUL
gee-tee-wee

Rabaa Kalish Sumar ~ #21
UNLEASH AND DEVELOP YOUR CREATIVE & ARTISTIC ABILITIES
rah-bah kah-leesh sue-mar

QSun ~ 24
MAKE PEOPLE WARMER TO YOU
cue-sun

PRAISE

ANGEL JELONCIA (f)
jell-ohn-see-uh
#112

JAMOVASAN ~ #1
BECOME MORE LOVING AND LOVABLE
jah-mo-vah-sahn

HOOVAUSH ~ #5
BECOME LESS CRITICAL
who-vawsh

ZOICE EXTOOZAR ~ #13
TURN YOUR WEAKNESS INTO YOUR STRENGTH
zoyce ex-too-zar

SKOZ SKALAM ~ #51
STOP THINKING NEGATIVE THOUGHTS
skoz skah-lam

PRECOGNITION

ANGEL WASADRIYE (m)
wah-saud-ree-yay
#103

Zdelanda ~ #6
BECOME MORE DISCERNING
zee-deh-lahn-dah

Kazeez Vontour ~ #11
INCREASE YOUR ABILITY TO FOCUS ON A TASK
kah-zeez vohn-tour

Vrans Xeka Korbose ~ #42
COMMUNICATE WITH YOUR HIGHER SELF USING
AUTOMATIC WRITING
vrans zee-kah core-bohs

Zonta Varbon ~ #89
COALESCE, CONCENTRATE AND AMPLIFY YOUR
AURIC POWER
zohn-tuh var-bohn

PROTECTION

ANGEL AUSTELJA (f)
ohs-tell-sjah
#141

QOBAKON ~ #3
BECOME MORE SELF-CONFIDENT & EMPOWERED
qwhoh-bah-kon

ZAKA XERAMZEY ~ #81
INVOKE A CIRCLE OF PROTECTION FROM PSYCHIC
ATTACKS
zahl-ah zee-ram-zey

ZAKA WZRAMZEY ~ #82
INVOKE A CIRCLE OF PROTECTION FROM PHYSICAL
VIOLENCE
zahk-ah whiz-ram-zey

ZONTA VARBON ~ #89
COALESCE, CONCENTRATE AND AMPLIFY YOUR
AURIC POWER
zohn-tuh var-bohn

TA RA ZERRAM ~ #94
NEUTRALIZE NEGATIVE ENERGY
tah rah zehr-ahm

RELATIONSHIP HARMONY

ANGEL VESTASANIEL (f)
vehst-ah-sahn-ee-el
#113

JAMOVASAN ~ #1
BECOME MORE LOVING AND LOVABLE
jah-mo-vah-sahn

JAAZ VAASHTATAN ~ #2
BECOME MORE PASSIONATE
jahz vaash-ta-tahn

ZINGGNIZ ~ #4
BECOME MORE BALANCED
zing-guh-nihz

HOOVAUSH ~ #5
BECOME LESS CRITICAL
who-vawsh

Gaussa Sabo ~ #10
RELEASE USELESS GUILT OR SHAME
gaws-sah sah-bow

Zoice Extoozar ~ #13
TURN YOUR WEAKNESS INTO YOUR STRENGTH
zoyce ex-too-zar

QSun ~ #24
MAKE PEOPLE WARMER TO YOU
cue-sun

Valacot Jasuprom ~ #32
MOTIVATE SOMEONE TO BE MORE LOVING
val-ah-kot jah-sue-prahm

VALACOT KAZRUN ~ #33
MOTIVATE SOMEONE TO BECOME MORE UNDERSTANDING
val-ah-kot kahz-ruhn

RELEASE

ANGEL NAYALIEL (f)
ney-ah-lee-el
#12

Gaussa Sabo ~ #10
RELEASE USELESS GUILT OR SHAME
gaws-sah sah-bow

Zoice Extoozar ~ #13
TURN YOUR WEAKNESS INTO YOUR STRENGTH
zoyce ex-too-zar

Jael Aladawon ~ #47
DIMINISH ANXIETY, FEAR AND WORRY
jah-el ah-lahd-ah-whon

Jael Julanari ~ #49
LESSEN EMOTIONAL PAIN OF GRIEF AFTER A LOSS
jah-el zhul-ahn-ahr-ee

SKOZ SKALAM ~ #51
STOP THINKING NEGATIVE THOUGHTS
skoz skah-lam

LERYLCEON ~ #52
IMPROVE YOUR MOOD
lehryl-cee-on

SOOLASEE JA GRAASON ~ #55
HEAL YOUR HEART FROM AN EMOTIONAL WOUND
soo-lah-see jah grah-sohn

AASHKADAR KURAZ ~ #62
SLEEP PEACEFULLY AND GET A GOOD NIGHT'S REST
ahsh-kah-dar coo-rahz

HAVATOR BLAASH ~ #66
ERASE A MEMORY YOU DO NOT WISH TO REMEMBER
hahv-ah-tour blaash

RESONANCE

Angel Vaalderyn (f)
vah-ahl-dur-in
#62

QOBAKON ~ #3
BECOME MORE SELF-CONFIDENT & EMPOWERED
qwhoh-bah-kon

ZINGGNIZ ~ #4
BECOME MORE BALANCED
zing-guh-nihz

ZDELANDA ~ #6
BECOME MORE DISCERNING
zee-deh-lahn-dah

YONTONA VAUSHAUN QZA ~ #41
BECOME MORE AWARE OF AND COMPREHENDING
OF A PERSON'S AURA
yohn-tah-nah vawsh-awn cue-zah

RESPECT

ANGEL ALEIFRDR (m)
ahl-layf-rder
#118

QOBAKON ~ #3
BECOME MORE SELF-CONFIDENT & EMPOWERED
qwhoh-bah-kon

QOVOOKA ~ #7
GAIN MORE SELF RESPECT
qwhoh-voo-kah

GAUSSA SABO ~ #10
RELEASE USELESS GUILT OR SHAME
gaws-sah sah-bow

ZOICE EXTOOZAR ~ #13
TURN YOUR WEAKNESS INTO YOUR STRENGTH
zoyce ex-too-zar

QUIALANTRA KA ~ #72
BECOME MORE INTELLIGENT AND RETAIN
KNOWLEDGE EASIER
ki-ah-lahn-trah kah

QWASATAR KA ~ #74
EASILY LEARN A NEW SKILL OR TALENT
kwah-suh-tar kah

ROMANTIC LOVE

Angel Vellusia (f)
vell-loo-cee-uh
#114

JAMOVASAN ~ #1
BECOME MORE LOVING AND LOVABLE
jah-mo-vah-sahn

JAAZ VAASHTATAN ~ #2
BECOME MORE PASSIONATE
jahz vaash-ta-tahn

JEETEEWEE ~ #8
BECOME MORE SPONTANEOUS & PLAYFUL
gee-tee-wee

JATAHSH LORNEY ~ #26
ATTRACT A ROMANTIC RELATIONSHIP
jah-tahsh lorn-ey

Wispaun Hookamba Sai ~ 40
BECOME MORE EMPATHETIC
whis-pawn who-kahm-bah say

Barkalon Dee ~ #44
MAGNIFY YOUR INTUITION
bark-ah-lon dee

SELF CONFIDENCE

ANGEL RALCHOSABAR (m)

rahl-choh-sah-bahr

#13

QOBAKON ~ #3
BECOME MORE SELF-CONFIDENT & EMPOWERED
qwhoh-bah-kon

ZINGGNIZ ~ #4
BECOME MORE BALANCED
zing-guh-nihz

QOVOOKA ~ #7
GAIN MORE SELF RESPECT
qwhoh-voo-kah

GAUSSA SABO ~ #10
RELEASE USELESS GUILT OR SHAME
gaws-sah sah-bow

ZOICE EXTOOZAR ~ #13
TURN YOUR WEAKNESS INTO YOUR STRENGTH
zoyce ex-too-zar

QUIALANTRA KA ~ #72
BECOME MORE INTELLIGENT AND RETAIN
KNOWLEDGE EASIER
ki-ah-lahn-trah kah

SELF LOVE

ANGEL LUXELLIOS (f)
luhks-el-lee-ohss
#14

QOBAKON ~ #3
BECOME MORE SELF-CONFIDENT & EMPOWERED
qwhoh-bah-kon

ZINGGNIZ ~ #4
BECOME MORE BALANCED
zing-guh-nihz

QOVOOKA ~ #7
GAIN MORE SELF RESPECT
qwhoh-voo-kah

GAUSSA SABO ~ #10
RELEASE USELESS GUILT OR SHAME
gaws-sah sah-bow

ZOICE EXTOOZAR ~ #13
TURN YOUR WEAKNESS INTO YOUR STRENGTH
zoyce ex-too-zar

VRANS XEKA KORBOSE ~ #42
COMMUNICATE WITH YOUR HIGHER SELF USING AUTOMATIC WRITING
vrans zee-kah core-bohs

SKOZ SKALAM ~ #51
STOP THINKING NEGATIVE THOUGHTS
skoz skah-lam

SLEEP

ANGEL SERTALEVA (f)
sehr-tah-lee-vah
#67

Zinggniz ~ #4
BECOME MORE BALANCED
zing-guh-nihz

Zoice Extoozar ~ #13
TURN YOUR WEAKNESS INTO YOUR STRENGTH
zoyce ex-too-zar

Ra Q Lon Baronde ~ #14
HAVE THE WILLPOWER TO RESIST TEMPTATION AND
OVERCOME BAD HABITS
rah cue lohn bah-ron-day

Zeeatar Yab ~ #15
BE MOTIVATED TO STOP PROCRASTINATING
zee-ahtar yahb

AASHKADAR KURAZ ~ #62
SLEEP PEACEFULLY AND GET A GOOD NIGHT'S REST
ahsh-kah-dar coo-rahz

SOUL MATES

ANGEL GUALNTHE (f)
goo-ahl-nth

#115

ZDELANDA ~ #6
BECOME MORE DISCERNING

zee-deh-lahn-dah

PEDLATZ ~ #19
REMEMBER AND INTERPRET YOUR DREAMS

ped-lahtz

JATAHSH LAADAKAND ~ #27
ATTRACT YOUR TRUE LOVE/SOUL MATE

jah-tahsh lah-dah-kahn-dah

YONTONA VAUSHAUN QZA ~ #41
BECOME MORE AWARE OF AND COMPREHENDING
OF A PERSON'S AURA

yohn-tah-nah vawsh-awn cue-zah

VRANS XEKA KORBOSE ~ #42
COMMUNICATE WITH YOUR HIGHER SELF USING
AUTOMATIC WRITING
vrans zee-kah core-bohs

BARKALON DEE ~ #44
MAGNIFY YOUR INTUITION
bark-ah-lon dee

SPIRITUAL AWAKENING

Angel Kadonacai (m)
kah-don-ah-kye
#129

Zdelanda ~ #6
BECOME MORE DISCERNING
zee-deh-lahn-dah

Elohim Jakaxe ~ #12
INCREASE YOUR SPIRITUALITY & CLOSENESS TO THE DIVINE
el-oh-heem jah-ka-zee

Zoice Extoozar ~ #13
TURN YOUR WEAKNESS INTO YOUR STRENGTH
zoyce ex-too-zar

Pedlatz ~ #19
REMEMBER AND INTERPRET YOUR DREAMS
ped-lahtz

292

Jataash Wiseef ~ #22
ATTRACT PEOPLE INTO YOUR LIFE THAT CAN HELP YOU
jah-tahsh whis-eef

Vrans Xeka Korbose ~ #42
COMMUNICATE WITH YOUR HIGHER SELF USING AUTOMATIC WRITING
vrans zee-kah core-bohs

STEWARDSHIP

ANGEL DAHLSHABON (m)
dahlz-shah-bahn
#63

JAAZ VAASHTATAN ~ #2
BECOME MORE PASSIONATE
jahz vaash-ta-tahn

ZEEATAR YAB ~ #15
BE MOTIVATED TO STOP PROCRASTINATING
zee-ahtar yahb

VRANS XEKA KORBOSE ~ #42
COMMUNICATE WITH YOUR HIGHER SELF USING
AUTOMATIC WRITING
vrans zee-kah core-bohs

SURVIVAL

ANGEL ELKAZAR (m)
el-kuh-zar
#143

ZINGGNIZ ~ #4
BECOME MORE BALANCED
zing-guh-nihz

ZDELANDA ~ #6
BECOME MORE DISCERNING
zee-deh-lahn-dah

KAZEEZ VONTOUR ~ #11
INCREASE YOUR ABILITY TO FOCUS ON A TASK
kah-zeez vohn-tour

ZOICE EXTOOZAR ~ #13
TURN YOUR WEAKNESS INTO YOUR STRENGTH
zoyce ex-too-zar

Jael Aladawon ~ #47
DIMINISH ANXIETY, FEAR AND WORRY
jah-el ah-lahd-ah-whon

Jael Omericsol ~ #50
DIMINISH PHYSICAL PAIN
jah-el o-mehr-ick-sohl

Skoz Skalam ~ #51
STOP THINKING NEGATIVE THOUGHTS
skoz skah-lam

Elohim Ootame ~ #80
GAIN WHATEVER YOU NEED TO OVERCOME AN
EMERGENCY
el-oh-heem oo-tah-mee

VOLONDO PARTANA ~ #88
RAPIDLY CHANGE YOUR LIFE'S REALITY
voh-lohn-dah pahr-tahn-ah

SUSTENANCE

ANGEL PELIAZEL (m)
pell-lee-uh-zell
#144

Ishshatar ~ #9
INCREASE YOUR LUCK
ish-shah-tar

Zoice Extoozar ~ #13
TURN YOUR WEAKNESS INTO YOUR STRENGTH
zoyce ex-too-zar

Jael Aladawon ~ #47
DIMINISH ANXIETY, FEAR AND WORRY
jah-el ah-lahd-ah-whon

Elohim Ootame ~ #80
GAIN WHATEVER YOU NEED TO OVERCOME AN
EMERGENCY
el-oh-heem oo-tah-mee

TELEKINESIS

ANGEL JARMION (m)
jar-mee-on
#104

Kazeez Vontour ~ #11
INCREASE YOUR ABILITY TO FOCUS ON A TASK
kah-zeez vohn-tour

Skoz Skalam ~ #51
STOP THINKING NEGATIVE THOUGHTS
skoz skah-lam

Qwasatar Ka ~ #74
EASILY LEARN A NEW SKILL OR TALENT
kwah-suh-tar kah

Zonta Varbon ~ #89
COALESCE, CONCENTRATE AND AMPLIFY YOUR AURIC POWER
zohn-tuh var-bohn

TELEPATHY

ANGEL KORBON (m)
kor-bawn
#105

ZDELANDA ~ #6
BECOME MORE DISCERNING
zee-deh-lahn-dah

KAZEEZ VONTOUR ~ #11
INCREASE YOUR ABILITY TO FOCUS ON A TASK
kah-zeez vohn-tour

ZOICE EXTOOZAR ~ #13
TURN YOUR WEAKNESS INTO YOUR STRENGTH
zoyce ex-too-zar

YONTONA VAUSHAUN QZA ~ #41
BECOME MORE AWARE OF AND COMPREHENDING
OF A PERSON'S AURA
yohn-tah-nah vawsh-awn cue-zah

Vava Kadong ~ 43
KNOW OTHER PEOPLE'S THOUGHTS
vah-vah kuh-dong

Qwasatar Ka ~ #74
EASILY LEARN A NEW SKILL OR TALENT
kwah-suh-tar kah

Zonta Varbon ~ #89
COALESCE, CONCENTRATE AND AMPLIFY YOUR
AURIC POWER
zohn-tuh var-bohn

TIME

ANGEL KHRONOSIOS (m)
crow-noh-see-ohs
#106

QOBAKON ~ #3
BECOME MORE SELF-CONFIDENT & EMPOWERED

qwhoh-bah-kon

ZINGGNIZ ~ #4
BECOME MORE BALANCED

zing-guh-nihz

ZDELANDA ~ #6
BECOME MORE DISCERNING

zee-deh-lahn-dah

KAZEEZ VONTOUR ~ #11
INCREASE YOUR ABILITY TO FOCUS ON A TASK

kah-zeez vohn-tour

Zoice Extoozar ~ #13
TURN YOUR WEAKNESS INTO YOUR STRENGTH
zoyce ex-too-zar

Khronos Loquar Viviel ~ #18
BE ABLE TO ACCOMPLISH MORE IN LESS TIME
crow-nose loh-kwawr viv-ee-el

Aashkadar Kuraz ~ #62
SLEEP PEACEFULLY AND GET A GOOD NIGHT'S REST
ahsh-kah-dar coo-rahz

TRANSITION

ANGEL LHYRSANTHE (f)
lye-ur-sahn-th
#64

GAUSSA SABO ~ #10
RELEASE USELESS GUILT OR SHAME
gaws-sah sah-bow

KAZEEZ VONTOUR ~ #11
INCREASE YOUR ABILITY TO FOCUS ON A TASK
kah-zeez vohn-tour

ZOICE EXTOOZAR ~ #13
TURN YOUR WEAKNESS INTO YOUR STRENGTH
zoyce ex-too-zar

JAEL ALADAWON ~ #47
DIMINISH ANXIETY, FEAR AND WORRY
jah-el ah-lahd-ah-whon

LERYLCEON ~ #52
IMPROVE YOUR MOOD
lehryl-cee-on

AASHKADAR KURAZ ~ #62
SLEEP PEACEFULLY AND GET A GOOD NIGHT'S REST
ahsh-kah-dar coo-rahz

TRUE FRIENDS

ANGEL CLISIDIS (m)
clee-see-dihs
#116

Jataash Wiseef ~ #22
ATTRACT PEOPLE INTO YOUR LIFE THAT CAN HELP
YOU
jah-tahsh whis-eef

Eizenhaar dlashmic ~ #25
ENCOURAGE NEW HARMONIOUS FRIEDSHIPS
eye-zen-haar dlash-mic

Jataash Mirakonda ~ #53
ATTRACT MORE POSITIVE AND SUPPORTIVE
FRIENDS INTO YOUR LIFE
jah-tahsh meer-ah-conda

TRUTH

ANGEL LEHONA (f)
lay-hoh-nah
#65

QOBAKON ~ #3
BECOME MORE SELF-CONFIDENT & EMPOWERED
qwhoh-bah-kon

ZINGGNIZ ~ #4
BECOME MORE BALANCED
zing-guh-nihz

ZDELANDA ~ #6
BECOME MORE DISCERNING
zee-deh-lahn-dah

GAUSSA SABO ~ #10
RELEASE USELESS GUILT OR SHAME
gaws-sah sah-bow

JATAASH WISEEF ~ #22
ATTRACT PEOPLE INTO YOUR LIFE THAT CAN HELP
YOU
jah-tahsh whis-eef

QPOC SALEEN ~ #37
REVEAL A PERSON'S HIDDEN AGENDA
cue-pock sah-leen

VAVA KADONG ~ 43
KNOW OTHER PEOPLE'S THOUGHTS
vah-vah kuh-dong

UNCONDITIONAL LOVE

ANGEL SHEZARLI (f)
shee-zar-lee
#119

JAMOVASAN ~ #1
BECOME MORE LOVING AND LOVABLE
jah-mo-vah-sahn

ZINGGNIZ ~ #4
BECOME MORE BALANCED
zing-guh-nihz

HOOVAUSH ~ #5
BECOME LESS CRITICAL
who-vawsh

SKOZ SKALAM ~ #51
STOP THINKING NEGATIVE THOUGHTS
skoz skah-lam

SOOLASEE JA GRAASON ~ #55
HEAL YOUR HEART FROM AN EMOTIONAL WOUND
soo-lah-see jah grah-sohn

VENTURES

ANGEL AHNSOVALD (f)
ahn-soh-vahld
#25

QOBAKON ~ #3
BECOME MORE SELF-CONFIDENT & EMPOWERED
qwhoh-bah-kon

ISHSHATAR ~ #9
INCREASE YOUR LUCK
ish-shah-tar

KAZEEZ VONTOUR ~ #11
INCREASE YOUR ABILITY TO FOCUS ON A TASK
kah-zeez vohn-tour

ZOICE EXTOOZAR ~ #13
TURN YOUR WEAKNESS INTO YOUR STRENGTH
zoyce ex-too-zar

ZEEATAR YAB ~ #15
BE MOTIVATED TO STOP PROCRASTINATING
zee-ahtar yahb

KHRONOS LOQUAR VIVIEL ~ #18
BE ABLE TO ACCOMPLISH MORE IN LESS TIME
crow-nose loh-kwawr viv-ee-el

JATAASH WISEEF ~ #22
ATTRACT PEOPLE INTO YOUR LIFE THAT CAN HELP
YOU
jah-tahsh whis-eef

VRANS XEKA KORBOSE ~ #42
COMMUNICATE WITH YOUR HIGHER SELF USING
AUTOMATIC WRITING
vrans zee-kah core-bohs

Jael Aladawon ~ #47
DIMINISH ANXIETY, FEAR AND WORRY
jah-el ah-lahd-ah-whon

Fjar Skos ~ #67
PROPEL YOUR BUSINESS OR PROJECT TO TAKE OFF
fuhjahr skoss

Quialantra Ka ~ #72
BECOME MORE INTELLIGENT AND RETAIN
KNOWLEDGE EASIER
ki-ah-lahn-trah kah

Steeka ~ #75
BE BETTER ORGANIZED
stee-kah

VIRTUE

ANGEL QUAN YIN (f)
kwan-yin
#90

JAMOVASAN ~ #1
BECOME MORE LOVING AND LOVABLE
jah-mo-vah-sahn

HOOVAUSH ~ #5
BECOME LESS CRITICAL
who-vawsh

GAUSSA SABO ~ #10
RELEASE USELESS GUILT OR SHAME
gaws-sah sah-bow

ELOHIM JAKAXE ~ #12
INCREASE YOUR SPIRITUALITY & CLOSENESS TO THE DIVINE
el-oh-heem jah-ka-zee

Vrans Xeka Korbose ~ #42
COMMUNICATE WITH YOUR HIGHER SELF USING
AUTOMATIC WRITING
vrans zee-kah core-bohs

Jataash Mirakonda ~ #53
ATTRACT MORE POSITIVE AND SUPPORTIVE
FRIENDS INTO YOUR LIFE
jah-tahsh meer-ah-conda

VISION

ANGEL ZHARRAIES (m)
zhair-reyes
#26

KAZEEZ VONTOUR ~ #11
INCREASE YOUR ABILITY TO FOCUS ON A TASK
kah-zeez vohn-tour

HUMAR RABATZ Q ~ #20
BECOME A LUCID DREAMER
hoo-mar rah-bats cue

VRANS XEKA KORBOSE ~ #42
COMMUNICATE WITH YOUR HIGHER SELF USING
AUTOMATIC WRITING
vrans zee-kah core-bohs

ZONTA VARBON ~ #89
COALESCE, CONCENTRATE AND AMPLIFY YOUR
AURIC POWER
zohn-tuh var-bohn

WELLNESS

ANGEL SÁLÁN (f)
sah-lahn
#72

ZINGGNIZ ~ #4
BECOME MORE BALANCED
zing-guh-nihz

ZOICE EXTOOZAR ~ #13
TURN YOUR WEAKNESS INTO YOUR STRENGTH
zoyce ex-too-zar

RA Q LON BARONDE ~ #14
HAVE THE WILLPOWER TO RESIST TEMPTATION AND
OVERCOME BAD HABITS
rah cue lohn bah-ron-day

AASHKADAR KURAZ ~ #62
SLEEP PEACEFULLY AND GET A GOOD NIGHT'S REST
ahsh-kah-dar coo-rahz

WILL POWER

ANGEL TIRUSAH (f)
tee-roo-sah
#15

Qovooka ~ #7
GAIN MORE SELF RESPECT
qwhoh-voo-kah

Gaussa Sabo ~ #10
RELEASE USELESS GUILT OR SHAME
gaws-sah sah-bow

Kazeez Vontour ~ #11
INCREASE YOUR ABILITY TO FOCUS ON A TASK
kah-zeez vohn-tour

Zoice Extoozar ~ #13
TURN YOUR WEAKNESS INTO YOUR STRENGTH
zoyce ex-too-zar

RA Q LON BARONDE ~ #14
HAVE THE WILLPOWER TO RESIST TEMPTATION AND
OVERCOME BAD HABITS
rah cue lohn bah-ron-day

ZEEATAR YAB ~ #15
BE MOTIVATED TO STOP PROCRASTINATING
zee-ahtar yahb

SKOZ SKALAM ~ #51
STOP THINKING NEGATIVE THOUGHTS
skoz skah-lam

JATAASH MIRAKONDA ~ #53
ATTRACT MORE POSITIVE AND SUPPORTIVE
FRIENDS INTO YOUR LIFE
jah-tahsh meer-ah-conda

341

FINAL THOUGHTS

Experienced practitioners of Celestine Light magick know from personal experience that they are working with very powerful, fast acting magick that can affect all aspects of life. It behooves those of us granted this knowledge to ever be cognizant of why and how Celestine Light Magick is so potent. It's foundation is in the light. It issues forth from the divine and pervades all of the universe, ever ready to be called into action by those who understand its secrets. As practitioners we are merely conduits for forces far more powerful than we can imagine; truly limitless when the purpose is selfless and noble.

The sigils and words of power we use are not from mere mortals on Earth. They come from far higher realms and are given to us to use with prudence and wisdom. The incantations we speak when casting a spell or an enchantment use rhyme and concise wording to call in and immensely amplify angelic and divine energies that can overcome all barriers, and vanquish all darkness.

In the course of your practice of Celestine Light magick, be ever mindful of its spiritual foundation in the light and your attunement and harmony with that foundation. You will be called upon to heal the sick, defend the defenseless, and purge negative energies and entities from both people and places. Whatever challenges of the darkness you are called upon to vanquish, always remember that manifestations of darkness, no matter how pervasive or seeming to be in control, will wither and vanish when confronted with the power of the light.

Darkness can only exist when there is little or no light. When the light radiates its brilliance, the darkness retreats and disappears. It has no choice. It has no recourse. No matter how dense, how pervasive, how evil and destructive, when the light fights back, the darkness has no defense;

like turning on a light bulb in a darkened room. There is nothing the darkness can do to usurp the light. It is only when the light chooses to not shine, to not defend, to not assert its power, that the darkness can return and dominate.

Remember my brothers and sisters who wield the magick of Celestine Light, you are the light. You are love. You are compassion. You are faith. You are honest and fair, and you are justice. Let your light forever shine!

Namaste,

Embrosewyn

PS If you have enjoyed and benefited from this book, I would be grateful if you would take a couple of minutes to go back to the book page on Amazon and leave a review.

OTHER CAPTIVATING, THOUGHT-PROVOKING BOOKS BY EMBROSEWYN

ANGELS OF MIRACLES AND MANIFESTATION
144 Names, Sigils and Stewardships To Call the Magickal Angels of Celestine Light

You are not alone. Whatever obstacle or challenge you face, whatever threat or adversary looms before you, whatever ability you seek to gain or mountain of life you want to conquer, divine angelic help is ready to intervene on your behalf. When the unlimited power of magickal angels stand with you, obstacles become opportunities, low times become springboards for better days, relationships blossom, illness becomes wellness, challenges become victories and miracles happen!

In *Angels of Miracles and Manifestation*, best-selling spiritual, magickal and paranormal author Embrosewyn Tazkuvel, reveals the secrets to summoning true magickal angels. And once called, how to use their awesome divine power to transform your compelling needs and desires into manifested reality.

Angel magick is the oldest, most powerful and least understood of all methods of magick. Ancient books of scripture from multiple religions tell of the marvelous power and miracles of angels. But the secrets of the true angel names, who they really are, their hierarchy, their stewardship responsibilities, their sigils, and how to successfully call them and have them work their divine magick for you, was lost to the world as a large part of it descended into the dark ages.

But a covenant was made by the Archangel Maeádael to the Adepts of Magick that as the people of the world evolved to a higher light the knowledge and power of angels would come again to the earth during the time of the Generation of Promise. That time is now. We are the Generation of Promise that has been foretold of for millennium. And all that was lost has been restored.

It doesn't matter what religion or path of enlightenment and empowerment that you travel: Wicca, Christianity, Pagan, Jewish, Buddhist, Occult, Muslim, Kabbalah, Vedic, something else or none at all. Nor does your preferred system of magick from Enochian, Thelemic, Gardnerian, Hermetic, to Tantric matter. Once you know the true names of the mighty angels, their unique sigils, and the simple but specific way to summon them, they will come and they will help you.

This revealing book of the ancient Celestine Light magick gives you immediate access to the divine powers of 14 Archangels, 136 Stewardship Angels, and hundreds of Specialty Angels that serve beneath them. Whether you are a novice or a magickal Adept you will find that when angels are on your side you manifest results that you never imagined possible except in your dreams.

The angel magick of Celestine Light is simple and direct without a lot of ritual, which makes it easy even for the novice to be able to quickly use it and gain benefit. While there is a place and importance to ritual in other types of magickal conjuring it is not necessary with angels. They are supernatural beings of unlimited power and awareness whose stewardship includes responding quickly to people in need who call upon them. You do not need elaborate rituals to get their attention.

If you are ready to have magick come alive in your life; if you are ready for real-life practical results that bring wisdom, happiness, health, love and abundance; if you are ready to unveil your life's purpose and unleash your own great potential, obtain the treasure that is this book. Call upon the magickal angels and they will come. But be prepared. When you summon angels, the magick happens and it is transformative. Your life will improve in ways big and small. But it will never be the same.

Want to know more? Take a moment to click on the Look Inside tab in the upper left of this page to see the full extent of the marvels that await you inside this book!

WORDS OF POWER AND TRANSFORMATION
101+ Magickal Words and Sigils of Celestine Light To Manifest Your Desires

Whatever you seek to achieve or change in your life, big or small, Celestine Light magickal words and sigils can help your sincere desires become reality.

Drawing from an ancient well of magickal power, the same divine source used by acclaimed sorcerers, witches and spiritual masters through the ages, the 101+ magickal words and sigils are revealed to the public for the very first time. They can create quick and often profound improvements in your life.

It doesn't matter what religion you follow or what you believe or do not believe. The magickal words and sigils are like mystical keys that open secret doors regardless of who holds the key. If you put the key in and turn it, the door will open and the magick will swirl around you!

From the beginner to the Adept, the Celestine Light words of power and sigils will expand your world and open up possibilities that may have seemed previously unachievable. Everything from something simple like finding a lost object, to something powerful like repelling a psychic or physical attack, to something of need such as greater income, to something life changing like finding your Soul Mate.

Some may wonder how a few spoken words combined with looking for just a moment at a peculiar image could have such immediate and often profound effects. The secret is these are ancient magick words of compelling power and the sigils are the embodiment of their magickal essence. Speaking or even thinking the words, or looking at or even picturing the sigil in your mind, rapidly draws angelic and magickal energies to you like iron to a magnet to fulfill the worthy purpose you desire.

This is a book of potent white magick of the light. Without a lot of training or ritual, it gives you the ability to overcome darkness threatening you from inside or out. For what is darkness except absence of the light? When light shines, darkness fades and disappears, not with a roar, but with a whimper.

Use the words and sigils to call in the magickal energies to transform and improve your life in every aspect. In this comprehensive book you will find activators to propel your personal growth, help you excel in school, succeed in your own business, or launch you to new heights in your profession. It will give you fast acting keys to improve your relationships, change your luck, revitalize your health, and develop and expand your psychic abilities.

Embrosewyn Tazkuvel is an Adept of the highest order in Celestine Light. After six decades of using magick and teaching it to others he is now sharing some of the secrets of what he knows with you. Knowledge that will instantly connect you to divine and powerful universal forces that with harmonic resonance, will unleash the magickal you!

Inside you will discover:

101 word combinations that call in magickal forces like a whirlwind of light.

177 magickal words in total.

101 sigils to go with each magickal word combination to amplify the magickal results you seek.

101 audio files you can listen to; helping you have perfect pronunciation of the Words of Power regardless of your native language. Available directly from the eBook and with a link in the paperback edition.

AURAS
How To See, Feel & Know

Auras: How to See, Feel & Know, **is like three books in one!**

1. It's an information packed, full color, complete training manual with 17 time tested exercises and 47 photos and illustrations to help you quickly be able to see Auras in vibrant color! It is the only full color book on auras available.

2. An entertaining read as Embrosewyn recalls his early childhood and high school experiences seeing auras, and the often humorous reactions by everyone from his mother to his friends when he told them what he saw.

3. Plus, a fascinating chapter on body language. Embrosewyn teaches in his workshops to not just rely on your interpretation of the aura alone, but to confirm it with another indicator such as body language.*Auras: How to See, Feel & Know*, goes in depth with thorough explanations and great pictures to show you all the common body language indicators used to confirm what someone's aura is showing you.

Auras includes:
- 17 dynamic eye exercises to help you rapidly begin to see the beautiful world of auras!
- 47 full color pictures and illustrations.

Anyone with vision in both eyes can begin seeing vividly colored auras around any person with just 5 minutes of practice!
Learn how to:
- See the 7 layers of the aura using Embrosewyn's pioneering technique
- Understand the meaning of the patterns and shadows observed in the layers
- Train your eyes to instantly switch back and forth from aura to normal vision
- Understand the meaning and nuances of every color of the rainbow in an aura
- Use your aura as a shield against negative energy or people
- Power up your aura to have greater achievement in any endeavor
- Interpret body language to confirm observations of the aura
- Cut negative energy cords to disharmonious people

- Understand health conditions and ailments through the aura

The secret to aura sight is to retrain the focusing parts of your eyes to see things that have always been there, but you have never been able to see before. It's really not complicated. Anyone can do it using Embrosewyn's proven techniques and eye exercises. The author has been seeing brightly colored auras for over 60 years and teaching others to begin seeing auras within 5 minutes for the last 22 years. *Auras: How to See, Feel & Know*, includes all the power techniques, tools and Full Color eye exercises from his popular workshops.

For those who already have experience seeing auras, the deeper auric layers and subtle auric nuances and the special ways to focus your eyes to see them, are explained in detail, with Full Color pictures andillustrations to show you how the deeper layers and auric aberrations appear. It is also a complete training manual to help you quickly be able to see Auras in vibrant color. It includes 17 eye exercises and dozens of Full Color pictures, enabling anyone with vision in both eyes to begin seeing vividly colored auras around any person. The secret is in retraining the focusing parts of your eyes to see things that have always been there, but you have never been able to see before. *Auras: How to See, Feel & Know*, includes all the power techniques, tools and Full Color eye exercises from Embrosewyn's popular workshops.

Additionally, there is a fascinating chapter on body language. Embrosewyn teaches in his workshops to not just rely on your interpretation of the aura alone, but to confirm it with another indicator such as body language. *Auras: How to See, Feel & Know* goes in depth with thorough explanations and great pictures to show you all the common body language indicators used to confirm what someone's aura is showing you.

For those who already have experience seeing auras, the deeper auric layers and subtle auric nuances and the special ways to focus your eyes to see them, are explained in detail, with accompanying Full Color pictures to show you how the deeper layers and auric aberrations appear

SOUL MATE AURAS
How To Find Your Soul Mate & "Happily Ever After"

The romantic dream of finding your Soul Mate, the person with whom you resonate on every level of your being, is more than a wishful notion. It is a deeply embedded, primal desire that persists on some level despite what may have been years of quiet, inner frustration and included relationships that while fulfilling on some levels, still fell short of the completeness of a Soul Mate.

Once found, your relationship with your Soul Mate can almost seem like a dream at times. It will be all you expected and probably much more. Having never previously had a relationship that resonated in harmony and expansiveness on every level of your being, you will have had nothing to prepare you for its wonder. Having never stood atop a mountain that tall with an expansiveness so exhilarating, once experienced, a committed relationship with your Soul Mate will give you a bliss and fulfillment such as you probably only imagined in fairy tales.

But how to find your Soul Mate? That is the million dollar question. The vast majority of people believe finding your Soul Mate is like a magnetic attraction, it will somehow just happen; in some manner you'll just be inevitably drawn to each other. The harsh reality is, 99% of people realize by their old age that it never happened. Or, if it did occur they didn't recognize their Soul Mate at the time, because they were looking for a different ideal.

Soul Mate Auras: How To Find Your Soul Mate & Happily Ever After gives you the master keys to unlock the passageway to discovering your Soul Mate using the certainty of your auric connections. Every person has a unique aura and auric field generated by their seven energy centers and their vitality. Find the person that you resonate strongly with on all seven energy centers and you'll find your Soul Mate!

Everyone can sense and see auras. In *Soul Mate Auras* full color eye and energy exercises will help you learn how to see and feel auras and how to use that ability to identify where in the great big world your Soul Mate is living. Once you are physically in the presence of your prospective Soul Mate, you will know how to use your aura to energetically confirm that they are the one. The same methods can be used to discover multiple people that are Twin Flames with you; not quite seven auric connection Soul Mates, but still deep and expansive connections to you on five to six energy centers.

Soul Mate Auras also includes an in-depth procedure to determine if someone is a Twin Flame or Soul Mate, not by using your aura, but by honestly and rationally evaluating your connections on all seven of your energy centers. This is an invaluable tool for anyone contemplating marriage or entering a long-term committed relationship. It also serves as a useful second opinion confirmation for anyone that has used their aura to find their Soul Mate.

To help inspire and motivate you to create your own "happily ever after," *Soul Mate Auras* is richly accentuated with dozens of full color photos of loving couples along with profound quotes from famous to anonymous people about the wonder of Soul Mates.

Treat yourself to the reality of finding your Soul Mate or confirming the one that you have already found! Scroll to the upper left of the page and click on Look Inside to find out more about what's inside this book!

Secret Earth Series
INCEPTION
Book 1

Could it be possible that there is a man alive on the Earth today that has been here for two thousand years? How has he lived so long? And why? What secrets does he know? Can his knowledge save the Earth or is it doomed?

Continuing the epic historical saga begun in the *Oracles of Celestine Light*, but written as a novel rather than a chronicle, *Inception* unveils the life and adventures of Lazarus of Bethany and his powerful and mysterious sister Miriam of Magdala.

The first book of the Secret Earth series, *Inception*, reveals the hidden beginnings of the strange, secret life of Lazarus. From his comfortable position as the master of caravans to Egypt he is swept into a web of intrigue involving his enigmatic sister Miriam and a myriad of challenging dangers that never seem to end and spans both space and time.

Some say Miriam is an angel, while others are vehement that she is a witch. Lazarus learns the improbable truth about his sister, and along with twenty-three other courageous men and women, is endowed with the secrets of immortality. But he learns that living the secrets is not as easy as knowing them. And living them comes at a price; one that needs to be paid in unwavering courage, stained with blood, built with toil, and endured with millenniums of sacrifice, defending the Earth from all the horrors that might have been. *Inception* is just the beginning of their odyssey.

DESTINY
Book 2

In preparation, before beginning their training as immortal Guardians of the Earth, Lazarus of Bethany and his wife Hannah were asked to go on a short visit to a world in another dimension. "Just to look around a bit and get a feel for the differences," Lazarus's mysterious sister, Miriam of Magdala assured them.

She neglected to mention the ravenous monstrous birds, the ferocious fire-breathing dragons, the impossibly perfect people with sinister ulterior motives, and the fact that they would end up being naked almost all the time! And that was just the beginning of the challenges!

UNLEASH YOUR PSYCHIC POWERS

A Comprehensive 400 Page Guidebook

Unleash Your Psychic Powers is an entertaining, enlightening and educational resource for all levels of practitioners in the psychic, magickal and paranormal arts. It includes easy-to-follow, step-by-step instructions on how you can develop and enhance the full potential of dynamic psychic, magickal and paranormal powers in your own life.

Whether You Are A Novice Or An Adept

You will find valuable insight and guidance, based upon Embrosewyn's six decades of experience discovering and developing psychic and paranormal talents and unleashing the power of the magickal arts.

Twenty Psychic And Paranormal Abilities Are Explored

Including well known abilities such as Clairvoyance, Telekinesis, Telepathy, Lucid Dreaming, Precognition, Astral Projection and Faith Healing, plus, more obscure talents such as Channeling, Dowsing, and Automatic Handwriting.

In addition to helping you develop and master the psychic abilities that call to you, each of the twenty powers described are spiced with fascinating personal stories from the lives of Embrosewyn and others, to help you understand some of the real world consequences and benefits of using these formidable magickal and psychic talents. Paranormal abilities have saved Embrosewyn's life and the lives of his family members on multiple occasions. Learning to fully develop your own psychic and paranormal abilities may come in just as handy one day.

For anyone that is an active spirit medium, or uses any psychic abilities involving other-worldly beings, such as divination, channeling, or ghost hunting, the chapter on Psychic Self-defense is an extensive must read, covering low, medium and high risk threats, including everything from negative vortexes, to entities, energy vampires, ghosts, aliens and demons. Exorcism, and how to protect both people and property from unseen forces is also completely explained.

Filled with pictures and vivid descriptions of how you can bring forth and develop your own transcendental supernatural gifts, *Unleash Your Psychic Powers* should be in the library of every serious student of the psychic, magickal, paranormal and supernatural.

Everyone has psychic and paranormal abilities. It is your birthright! You were born with them!

Within this book you'll learn how to unlock and unleash your astounding supernatural potential and the amazing things you can do with your powers once they are free!

LOVE YOURSELF
The Secret Key to Transforming Your Life

Loving yourself is all about energy

As humans we devote a great deal of our energy through our time, thoughts and emotions to love. We read about it, watch movies and shows about it, dream about it, hope for it to bless our lives, feel like something critically important is lacking when it doesn't, and at the very least keep a sharp eye out for it when its missing.

Too often we look to someone else to fulfill our love and crash and burn when relationships end, or fail to live up to our fantasies of what we thought they should be. When we seek love from another person or source greater than the love we give to ourselves, we set ourselves up to an inevitable hard landing when the other person or source ceases to provide the level of fulfillment we desire.

Loving yourself is a precious gift from you to you. It is an incredibly powerful energy that not only enhances your ability to give love more fully to others, it also creates a positive energy of expanding reverberation that brings more love, friendship and appreciation to you from all directions. It is the inner light that illuminates your life empowering you to create the kind of life you desire and dream.

The relationship you have with yourself is the most important one in your life. Happiness will forever be fleeting if you do not have peace, respect and love for yourself. It's not selfish. It's not vain. It is in fact the key to transforming your life. Inward reflection and appreciation will open up clearer channels to the divine. Relationships with everyone will be enhanced as your relationship with yourself expands and is uplifted.

All other relationships are only mirrors of the one you have within. As you love yourself, are kind to yourself, respect yourself, so too will you be able to give those and so many other good qualities to others in equal measure to that which you give to yourself.

This is a short, but very sweet book to help you discover your inner glow of love. Within its covers are two great keys you will find no other place. These two keys will proactively bring you to the serenity of self-love regardless of whether you are currently near or far from that place of peace.

Are you familiar with the infinity symbol? It looks pretty much like the number 8 turned on its side. As love for yourself should be now and forever, in the last chapter you will find 88 reasons why loving yourself is vitally important to your joy, personal growth and expansion, and the happiness of everyone whose lives you touch. Most people have never considered that there could be a list that long just about loving yourself! But with each short phrase you read your mind begins to understand to a greater depth how important loving yourself is for all aspects of your life and relationships. As your mind understands your life follows.

This book leaves you with a special gift Inside you'll find two short, but very valuable multimedia flash presentations. One is entitled "Forgive Yourself". The other is "Love Yourself" These are not normal flash presentations. They are self-hypnosis, positive affirmations that will rapidly help you achieve greater self-love and more fulfilling love-filled realities in your life. As soft repetitive music plays in the background, images reinforcing the theme will flash by on your screen about three per second, accompanied by short phrases superimposed on a portion of the image. In a quick 7-10 minute session, sitting at home in front of your computer, you will find the flash presentations buoy and motivate you. Repeat them twice a day for several days and you will find they are transformative.

Special Bonus: *Love Yourself* is ALSO AVAILABLE AS AN AUDIO BOOK! This allows you to listen and read at the same time!

PSYCHIC SELF DEFENSE

A Complete Guide to Protecting Yourself Against Psychic & Paranormal Attack (and just plain irksome people)

Felt a negative energy come over you for no apparent reason when you are near someone or around certain places? Had a curse hurled at you? Spooked by a ghost in a building? Imperiled by demonic forces? Being drained and discombobulated by an energy vampire? Or, do you encounter more mundane but still disruptive negative energies like an over demanding boss, the local bully, hurtful gossip, a physically or mentally abusive spouse, or life in a dangerous neighborhood threatened by thieves and violence? Whatever your source of negative energy, danger or threat, you'll find effective, proven, psychic and magickal countermeasures within this book.

Psychic Self Defense draws upon Embrosewyn's six decades of personal experience using psychic abilities and magickal defenses to thwart, counter and send back to sender, any and all hostile paranormal threats. Everything from unsupportive and dismissive family and friends, to ghosts, demons and exorcisms. The same practical and easy to learn Magickal techniques can be mastered by anyone serious enough to give it some time and practice, and can aid you immensely with a host of material world challenges as well.

17 psychic and paranormal threats are covered with exact, effective counter measures, including many real life examples from Embrosewyn's comprehensive personal experiences with the paranormal, devising what works and what doesn't from hard won trial and error.

Whether you are a medium needing to keep foul spirits away, or simply someone desiring to know that you, your family and property are safe and protected, you will find the means to insure peace and security with the proven methods outlined in *Psychic Self Defense*

You will learn how to:
- Create your own Magick spells tailored to your particular situation and need
- Call upon specific angels to aid you
- Create Crystal Energy Shields
- Protect yourself when in a channeling or spirit medium trance
- Use your Aura to create ASP's (Auric Shields of Power)

- Empower Wards for protection against specific threats
- Recognize and counter Energy Vampires
- Cleanse a home of negative energy
- Cut negative energy cords to disharmonious people
- Counter Black Magick
- Detect alien presence
- Banish malicious entities or demons

Though dealing with numerous and sometimes dangerous other-worldly and material world threats, the entire approach of this book is from a position of personal empowerment, no fear, and divine white light. Whether you are religious or an atheist, an experienced practitioner of the psychic and magickal arts or a neophyte, someone living in a haunted house or just an employee wanting to have a nicer boss, there will be hundreds of ways you can use the information in this book to help you in your life. And you will learn to do it in ways that are uplifting and empowering, producing results that are peaceful, safe and harmonious.

Psychic Self Defense is also available as an AUDIO BOOK.

22 STEPS TO THE LIGHT OF YOUR SOUL

A Treasured Book That Will Help You Unleash The Greatness Within

What would it be like if you could reach through space and time to query the accumulated wisdom of the ages and get an answer? *22 Steps to the Light of Your Soul*, reveals such treasured insights, eloquently expounding upon the foundational principles of 22 timeless subjects of universal interest and appeal, to help each reader grow and expand into their fullest potential.

In a thought-provoking, poetic writing style, answers to questions we all ponder upon, such as love, happiness, success and friendship, are explored and illuminated in short, concise chapters, perfect for a thought to ponder through the day or contemplate as your eyes close for sleep.

Each paragraph tells a story and virtually every sentence could stand alone as an inspiring quote on your wall.

These are the 22 steps of the Light of Your Soul

Step 1: The Purpose of Life

Step 2: Balance

Step 3: Character

Step 4: Habits

Step 5: Friendship

Step 6: True Love

Step 7: Marriage

Step 8: Children

Step 9: Happiness

Step 10: Play & Relaxation

Step 11: Health

Step 12: Success

Step 13: Knowledge

Step 14: Passion & Serenity

Step 15: Imagination & Vision

Step 16: Creativity & Art

Step 17: Adversity

Step 18: Respect

Step 19: Freedom & Responsibility

Step 20: Stewardship

Step 21: Faith

Step 22: Love Yourself - the Alpha and the Omega

22 Steps to the Light of Your Soul is also available as an AUDIO BOOK.

ORACLES OF CELESTINE LIGHT
Complete Trilogy Of Genesis, Nexus And Vivus

Once in a lifetime comes a book that can dramatically change your life for the better - forever. This is it!

WHAT WAS LOST...HAS BEEN FOUND

This is the complete 808 page trilogy of the Celestine books of Light: Genesis, Nexus and Vivus.

The controversial *Oracles of Celestine Light*, is a portal in time to the days of Yeshua of Nazareth, over 2000 years ago, revealed in fulfilling detail to the world by the reclusive Embrosewyn Tazkuvel. It includes 155 chapters of sacred wisdom, miracles and mysteries revealing life-changing knowledge about health, longevity, happiness and spiritual expansion that reverberates into your life today.

Learn the startling, never before understood truth:

About aliens, other dimensions, Atlantis, Adam & Eve, the Garden of Eden, Noah and the ark, giants, the empowerment of women, dreams, angels, Yeshua of Nazareth (Jesus), his crucifixion & resurrection, his wife Miriam of Magdala (Mary Magdala), Yudas Iscariot (Judas), the afterlife, reincarnation, energy vortexes, witches, magic, miracles, paranormal abilities, and you!

The *Oracles of Celestine Light* turns accepted religious history and traditional teachings on their head. But page by page, it makes more sense than anything you've ever read and shares simple yet profound truths to make your life better today and help you to understand and unleash your miraculous potential.

The *Oracles of Celestine Light* explains who you are, why you are here, and your divine destiny. It is a must-read for anyone interested in spirituality, personal growth and thought-provoking answers to the unknown.

"You are a child of God, a Child of Light, literally a priceless son or daughter of divinity. Even through the fog of mortal upheavals and the tumults and tribulations, always remember you are still a child of God and shall inherit joy and kingdoms beyond measure, as you remain true to your light." Genesis 11:99

Psychic Awakening Series
CLAIRVOYANCE

Would it be helpful if you could gain hidden knowledge about a person, place, thing, event, or concept, not by any of your five physical senses, but with visions and "knowing?"

Are you ready to supercharge your intuition? *Clairvoyance* takes you on a quest of self-discovery and personal empowerment, helping you unlock this potent ESP ability in your life. It includes riveting stories from Embrosewyn's six decades of psychic and paranormal adventures, plus fascinating accounts of others as they discovered and cultivated their supernatural abilities.

Clearly written, step-by-step practice exercises will help you to expand and benefit from your own psychic and clairvoyant abilities. This can make a HUGE improvement in your relationships, career and creativity. As Embrosewyn has proven from over twenty years helping thousands of students to find and develop their psychic and paranormal abilities, EVERYONE, has one or more supernatural gifts. *Clairvoyance* will help you discover and unleash yours!

If you are interested in helping yourself to achieve more happiness, better health, greater knowledge, increased wealth and a deeper spirituality, unlocking your power of clairvoyance can be the key. Hidden knowledge revealed becomes paths unseen unveiled.

Unleashing your psychic gifts does more than just give you advantage in life challenges. It is a safe, ethical, even spiritual and essential part of you that makes you whole, once you accept that you have these special psychic abilities and begin to use them.

TELEKINESIS

Easy, comprehensive guide for anyone wanting to develop the supernatural ability of Telekinesis

Telekinesis, also known as psychokinesis, is the ability to move or influence the properties of objects without physical contact. Typically it is ascribed as a power of the mind. But as Embrosewyn explains, based upon his sixty years of personal experience, the actual physical force that moves and influences objects emanates from a person's auric field. It initiates with a mental thought, but the secret to the power is in your aura!

Telekinesis is the second book in the Psychic Awakening series by popular paranormal writer Embrosewyn Tazkuvel. The series was specifically created to offer short, inexpensive, information filled handbooks to help you quickly learn and develop specific psychic and paranormal abilities.

Clearly written, *Telekinesis* is filled with step-by-step practice exercises and training techniques proven to help you unlock this formidable paranormal ability. Spiced with riveting accounts of real-life psychic experiences and paranormal adventures, you'll be entertained while you learn. But along the way you will begin to unleash the potent power of Telekinesis in your own life!

As Embrosewyn has proven from over twenty years helping thousands of students to find and develop their psychic and paranormal abilities. EVERYONE, has one or more supernatural gifts. Is Telekinesis one of yours? Perhaps it's time to find out.

DREAMS

Awaken in the world of your sleep

In *Dreams*, the third book of the Psychic awakening series, renowned psychic/paranormal practitioner Embrosewyn Tazkuvel reveals some of his personal experiences with the transformational effect of dreams, while sharing time-tested techniques and insights that will help you unlock the power of your own night travels.

Lucid Dreaming

An expanded section on Lucid Dreaming gives you proven methods to induce and develop your innate ability to control your dreams. It explores the astonishing hidden world of your dream state that can reveal higher knowledge, greatly boost your creativity, improve your memory, and help you solve vexing problems of everyday life that previously seemed to have no solution.

Nine Types of Dreams

Detailing the nine types of dreams will help you to understand which dreams are irrelevant and which you should pay close attention to, especially when they reoccur. You'll gain insight into how to interpret the various types of dreams to understand which are warnings and which are gems of inspiration that can change your life from the moment you awaken and begin to act upon that which you dreamed.

Become the master of your dreams

Sleeping and dreaming are a part of your daily life that cumulatively accounts for dozens of years of your total life. It is a valuable time of far more than just rest. Become the master of your dreams and your entire life can become more than you ever imagined possible. Your dreams are the secret key to your future.

Additional Services Offered by Embrosewyn

I am honored to be able to be of further service to you by offering multiple paranormal abilities for your enlightenment and life assistance. On a limited basis as my time allows I can:

- discover your Soul Name and the meaning and powers of the sounds
- custom craft and imbue enchantments upon a piece of your jewelry for a wide beneficial range of purposes
- discover the name of your Guardian Angel
- have an in-depth psychic consultation and Insight Card reading with you via a Skype video call.

My wife Sumara can also create a beautiful piece of collage art on 20"x30" internally framed canvas, representing all of the meanings and powers of the sounds of your Soul Name.

If you are interested in learning more about any f these additional services please visit my website: *www.embrosewyn.com* and click on the link at the top for SERVICES.

If you would like to purchase enchanted jewelry or gemstones for specific purposes such as love, health, good fortune, or psychic protection please visit my website: *www.magickalgems.com.*

For great info on a wide variety of psychic, paranormal and magick subjects, please visit my YouTube Channel, *Esoteric Mystery School with Embrosewyn Tazkuvel.*

Printed in the USA
CPSIA information can be obtained
at www.ICGtesting.com
LVHW020719070124
768171LV00083B/473/J